Builder's Essentials

Framing & Rough Carpentry

Second Edition

Scot Simpson

With original illustrations by
Gary Burhop

RSMeans
CMDGROUP

Builder's Essentials

Framing & Rough Carpentry

Second Edition

The Illustrated Guide for Apprentices & Carpenters

Scot Simpson

Copyright 2001

R.S. Means Company, Inc.
Construction Publishers & Consultants
Construction Plaza
63 Smiths Lane
Kingston, MA 02364-0800
(800) 334-3509

The editors for this book were Howard Chandler and Danielle Georges; managing editor was Mary Greene. The production manager was Michael Kokernak. The production coordinator was Marion Schofield. The electronic publishing specialist was Sheryl Rose. Robert Megerdichian was a contributing illustrator. The book and cover were designed by Norman R. Forgit.

Printed in the United States of America

10 9 8 7 6 5 4 3 2 1

Library of Congress Cataloging in Publication Data

ISBN 0-87629-617-7

Table of Contents

Chapter 5: Roof Framing

Chapter 6: Doors, Windows, and Stairs

Introduction

In 1991, the first edition of *Framing and Rough Carpentry* was published. Then, I was responding to the need for a textbook I could use in teaching my framer trainees the basics. I wanted them all to learn the same framing method to ensure that they would correctly interpret my instructions, and execute them with predictable and consistent results. I also wanted the text to be easy enough so that they could read and absorb its contents quickly. Finally, I wanted it to cover all aspects of the trade—from definitions of framing terms to guidelines for the management of a framing crew. What emerged was an easy-to-use outline of modern methods of framing.

In preparing this *second edition* of *Framing and Rough Carpentry,* I am surprised at how much is still the same—the basic framing concepts and systems stay the same. Some things, however, do change, and this edition covers changes in building code that occurred in 2000, and the trend toward one code, the International Building Code (IBC). With the exception of California, most states have adopted the IBC. This edition includes updated nailing patterns and specifications for pneumatic nails. There is also information on Engineered Wood Products which are becoming more and more a part of everyday framing. Another feature is the expanded section on work place safety and how to protect yourself from injuries in your job as a framer.

The second edition, like the first, was developed for framing contractors and framer trainees, but it can be used equally well by many others, including general carpenters, renovators, remodelers, and handymen—in short, by anyone interested in learning basic framing.

Prior to writing the first edition, I had framed structures in many states across the country (including 48 apartment projects, 9 condominium projects, 8 office buildings, 6 hotels, and 27 houses). I have since taught framing in Japan, Korea and the Czech Republic. I have also framed in Greece and Spain, and the first edition of this book has been translated into Japanese, Korean, the Queen's English (metric), and just last year into Chinese. Everywhere I went the first edition was the tool I used to communicate the basics of framing.

What I have tried to do in this second edition is draw from my more than 30 years of experience in framing, and bring together the best techniques from different parts of the country, setting a standard for my trainees and crews.

This manual is designed to be "Framer Friendly." I hope that you find it friendly to you.

SCOT SIMPSON

Chapter One

The Trade of Wood Framing

T he trade of wood framing is comprised of the rough carpentry skills needed to produce the "skeleton" of a building and its first layer of "skin." The skeleton consists of the structural lumber forming the floors, walls, and roof; the skin consists of the lumber which encloses the skeleton, and provides a surface for subsequent layers of protective and decorative finish materials.

This chapter is an illustrated review of a framer's most basic tools, materials, and terminology. This information is so basic that it usually is not even taught on the job site, so if you don't know it when you arrive for work, you will have to play a guessing game or ask a lot of questions.

The illustrations with terms serve as a handy reference, and help to reduce confusion when different words are used for the same item. Confusion can arise when framers move from job site to job site, and work with different people. For example, bottom plates are often known as *sole plates,* backers as *partitions*, and trimmers as *cripples*. But it doesn't matter what they are called as long as you know what they are. There is also a more detailed list of framing terms with definitions at the back of the book.

The suggested organization for a framing tool truck presented in this chapter is just an example of how a truck might be set up for tool storage. Its purpose is, once again, to reduce confusion and make the job easier. It is amazing how much time can be spent looking for tools and nails if they aren't put where a framer expects them to be.

Contents

Bearing Walls

Bearing walls support the main weight of an upper portion of a building, such as a ceiling, floor, or roof. Nonbearing walls provide little or no support to those upper portions. Remove nonbearing walls and the upper portions will stand; remove bearing walls and the upper portions will fall.

Nonbearing Walls

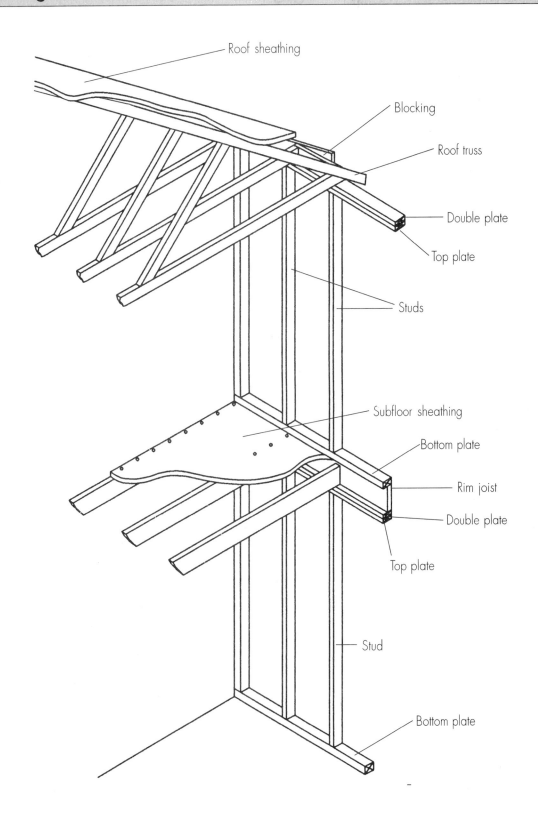

Roof sheathing

Blocking

Roof truss

Double plate

Top plate

Studs

Subfloor sheathing

Bottom plate

Rim joist

Double plate

Top plate

Stud

Bottom plate

Framing Lumber

Lumber is sized in "nominal," as opposed to "actual," dimensions. A nominal dimension rounds off the actual dimension to the next highest whole number. For example, a piece of lumber which actually measures 1½"× 3½" is rounded off to the nominal 2" × 4".

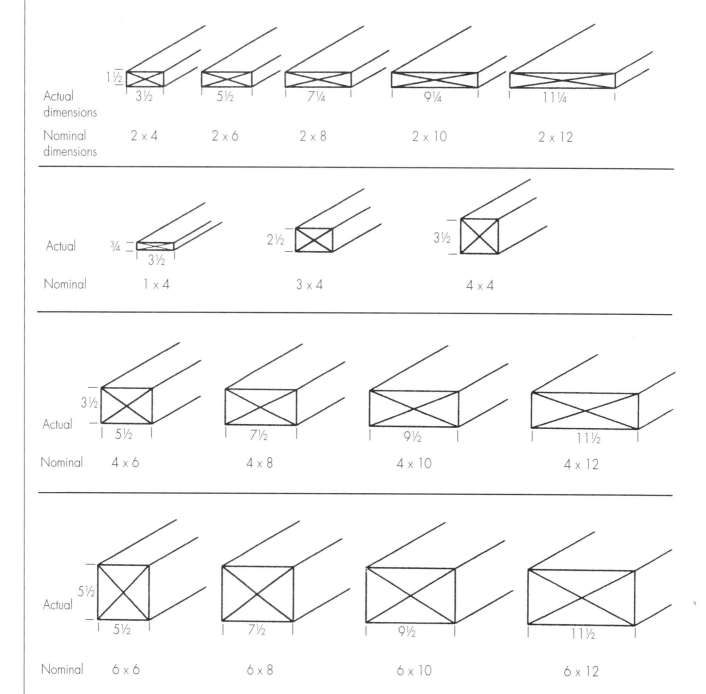

Actual dimensions	1½ × 3½	5½	7¼	9¼	11¼
Nominal dimensions	2 x 4	2 x 6	2 x 8	2 x 10	2 x 12

Actual	¾ × 3½	2½	3½	
Nominal	1 x 4	3 x 4	4 x 4	

Actual	3½ × 5½	7½	9½	11½
Nominal	4 x 6	4 x 8	4 x 10	4 x 12

Actual	5½ × 5½	7½	9½	11½
Nominal	6 x 6	6 x 8	6 x 10	6 x 12

4

Wood Structural Panels

½" sheet
⅝" sheet
¾" sheet

Sheathing comes in 4' × 8' sheets. The thicknesses most commonly used in framing are ½", ⅝", and ¾".

T&G Wood Structural Panels
(tongue and groove)

GWB

½" — GWB
⅝" — GWB

GWB = Gypsum wallboard (also called drywall or sheetrock). The most common thicknesses are ½" and ⅝".

Engineered Wood Products

Engineered Wood Products are becoming more and more a part of our everyday framing. The strengths of these different products vary. Whenever you use engineered wood, it is important that you understand the qualities of the specific product you are planning to use, as well as structural considerations and any restrictions on cutting and installation.

Engineered wood products can be divided into two categories: Engineered Panel Products and Engineered Lumber Products. Engineered Panel Products include plywood, oriented strand board (OSB), waferboard, composite and structural particleboard. Engineered Lumber Products include I-joists, Glu-lam beams, LVLs (laminated veneer lumber), PSLs (parallel strand lumber), and LSLs (laminated strand lumber).

Engineered wood products have structural qualities different than those of traditional wood, so they must be used within the specification set by the manufacturer. When these products are specified on the plans, the architect or engineer who specified them will have checked with his or her structural engineer to ensure proper use.

Engineered panel products have been around for years and are treated in a manner similar to engineered wood products. The 4' × 8' typical sheets are strongest in the direction of the grain. For floors and roofs, these sheets should be laid perpendicular to the direction of the supporting members. The strength of the panels is developed from the panel cantilevering over the supports and so each piece should be at least as long as two support members.

8'

4'

Plywood
½" sheet
⅝" sheet
¾" sheet

Wood strip, wood blocks, or lightweight concrete flooring.

Stagger (optional)

Leave space at all panel edge joints and $\frac{1}{8}$" space at all panel end joints unless otherwise recommended by panel manufacturer.

2x joists, plywood-webbed I-joists or floor trusses.

APA RATED SHEATHING

Long dimension

(Illustration courtesy of Trus Joist)

APA
RATED SHEATHING
32/16 15/32 INCH
SIZED FOR SPACING
EXPOSURE 1
000
NRB-108

Glu-lam beams, LVLs, PSLs, and LSLs can be cut to length, but should not be drilled or notched without checking with manufacturers' specifications.

I-joists are becoming more widely used. Although the Engineered Wood Association has a standard for I-joists, not all I-joists manufacturers subscribe to the standard. Consequently, it is important to follow the manufacturer's instructions whenever using I-joists. Installation instructions are usually delivered with the load for each job. The illustration shows some of the typical instructions.

Certain features are common among all I-joists. Rim and blocking may be of I-joist or solid rim board. Typical widths are 9½", 11⁷/₈", 14", 16", and 20". Web stiffeners are used to add to the strength at bearing points. If the bearing point is at the bottom flange, then the web stiffener, which is the thickness of the flange on one side of the web, is held tight to the bottom. There should be at least a ¹/₈" space between the top flange and the web stiffener. If the bearing point is at the top flange, then the web stiffener is held tight to the top with at least ¹/₈" between the bottom flange and the web stiffener.

Bridging or mid-span blocking is not required but may enhance floor performance if properly installed.

Safety strut lines (1×4 minimum) for stability during installation:
- TJI®/Pro™ 150 joists: 6' on-center maximum
- TJI®/Pro™ 250, 350 and 550 joists: 8' on-center maximum
- Fasten at each joist with 2-8d (2½") nails minimum

Joists must be laterally supported at cantilever and end bearings by blocking panels, hangers or direct attachment to a rim board or rim joist.

Braced end wall

Treated 2x_ ledger

Flashing

½" diameter lag bolts, 2" minimum from edge

Structural sheathing

Protect wood from direct contact with concrete

1½" knockouts at approximately 12" on-center

See hole charts in Trus Joist's current product literature for allowable web holes and required distances from support

Residential Floor Framing

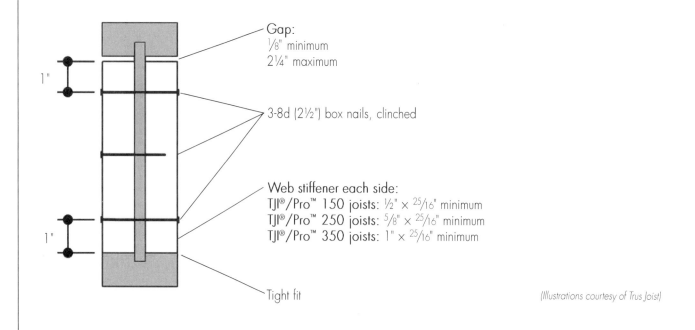

Gap:
⅛" minimum
2¼" maximum

1"

3-8d (2½") box nails, clinched

Web stiffener each side:
TJI®/Pro™ 150 joists: ½" × 25/16" minimum
TJI®/Pro™ 250 joists: ⅝" × 25/16" minimum
TJI®/Pro™ 350 joists: 1" × 25/16" minimum

1"

Tight fit

(Illustrations courtesy of Trus Joist)

Bottom Bearing

Squash blocks are used when additional strength is needed for point loads. They are typically dimensional lumber like 2 × 4s or 2 × 6s. They should be cut ¹/₁₆" longer than the I-joist to take the load off the I-joists.

I-joist hardware, such as hangers, are usually delivered with the I-joist package. However, standard I-joist hardware can be purchased separately.

I-joists typically require 1¾" bearing. You can cut the end of an I-joist as long as it is not cut beyond a line straight up from the end of the bearing.

In 1980, 50 million feet of I-joists were produced. It is estimated that in 2000, 900 million lineal feet were produced. This trend will probably continue, as it will with other existing and new engineered products.

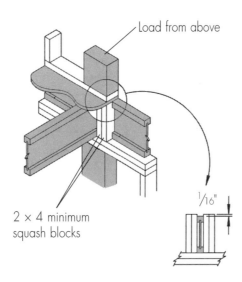

Load from above

2 × 4 minimum squash blocks

¹/₁₆"

I-joists

Rim board

DO NOT bevel cut joist beyond inside face of wall.

(Illustrations courtesy of Trus Joist)

Lumber and Wood Structural Panel Grades

Lumber and wood structural panels are graded for strength and different uses. Each piece of lumber is stamped for identification before it is shipped. Architects specify grades of lumber and wood structural panels for various purposes, and framers need to make sure the right wood is used.

Sample grade stamps

12 Ⓦ 2 S-DRY D/FIR

SPIB® No.2
KD19 ⑦

12 STAND
Ⓦ &BTR
WP® S-DRY D/FIR/S

(Stamps courtesy of Western Woods Production Assoc. & Southern Pine Inspection Bureau)

Framing	Grade	Use
Light framing 2 x 2 thru 4 x 4	Construction Standard & better Utility	Plates Sills Studs over 10'
Stud 2 x 2 thru 4 x 6 10' or less	Stud	Studs Cripples
Structural framing	Select structural No.1 No. 2 No. 3	Joists Rafters Headers Posts Beams

Type of wood, e.g., Douglas fir, Englemann spruce, Alpine fir, Southern Pine. Sometimes architects designate a specific type.

Western Wood Products, mill #12

Southern Pine Inspection Bureau mill #7

Maximum 19% moisture content
APA
The Engineered Wood Association

Specific designated construction application

Thickness

APA
THE ENGINEERED WOOD ASSOCIATION

RATED SHEATHING
24/16 7/16 INCH
SIZED FOR SPACING
EXPOSURE 1
000
PRP-108 HUD-UM-40

Maximum joist spacing for subflooring
Maximum rafter spacing for roofs

Exposure durability classification
(Check plans or specifications for architect's designation)

Classifications: —Exterior
                  —Exposure 1
                  —Exposure 2
                  —Interior

APA
THE ENGINEERED WOOD ASSOCIATION

A-C GROUP 1
EXTERIOR
000
PS 1-95

Face veneer grade
Back veneer grade
Grades: N – Highest quality "natural finish"
         A – High quality
         B – Sanded smooth
         C – Minimum grade for exterior
         D – Interior or weather-protected

(Stamps courtesy of APA– The Engineered Wood Association)

Framing Nails

Frequently Used Nails

16d*

16d Common – 3-½" long & .162" thick
16d Box – 3-½" long & .135" thick
16d Sinkers – 3-¼" long & .148" thick

3" x .131"

P-Nail – used in a pneumatic nail gun

8d

8d Common – 2-½" long & .131" thick
8d Box – 2-½" long & .113" thick
8d Sinkers – 2-³⁄₈" long & .113" thick

Sinkers have a countersunk checked head and a cement or vinyl coating for easy nailing

Inches

| 1 | 2 | 3 | 4 |

Joist hanger nail

Roofing nail

Concrete nail

Casing nail

*d = Penny. The abbreviation comes from the Roman word "denarius," meaning coin, which the English adapted to penny. It originally referred to the cost of a specific nail per 100. Today it refers only to nail size.

Framing Tools

Hammer

Tape

Utility knife

Chalk line

Speed square

Try square

Framing square

Marking crayon

Carpenter's pencil

Nail puller
or
Cat's paw

Chisel

Glue gun

Tool pouch

Electric cord

Crowbar

Wall puller

Air hose

Flat bar

Sledgehammer

Drill

Nail gun

Concrete nail gun

Reciprocating saw

Chain saw

Worm-drive saw
(Circular saw)

Air compressor

Router

Hand saw

Framing Tool Truck

Typical Layout for a 14' Step Van

Organizing your tools helps keep them in good condition and helps you find them when you need them, thereby saving valuable time on the job.

Accuracy in measuring, marking, and cutting lumber is a very important framing skill to master.

Periodic checks should be made of the condition for accuracy of tape measures and the squareness of saw tables and blades.

25'
Tape

Check to make sure tape end is not bent and that it moves on the end rivets.

Speed square

Use speed square to make sure saw table and saw blade are square with each other.

Saw blade

Saw upside down

A typical saw blade removes a channel of wood approximately ⅛" wide, called a "kerf." This must be taken into consideration when you make a cut.

Suppose you want to cut a board 25" long. Measure and make a mark at 25", then square a line through the mark with a try-square. The "work piece" — the 25" piece you want to use — will be to the left of the line; the "waste piece" will be to the right. Guide your saw along the right edge of the line so the kerf is made in the waste piece. If your cut is perfectly made, the work piece will be left showing exactly half the width of your pencil line, and will measure exactly 25". Thus, the old carpenter's saying: "Leave the line."

EX: Cut a 25" piece

Measure and mark

Work piece | Waste piece

Square a line through mark

⅛" kerf (saw blade cut)
Cut to the right of line

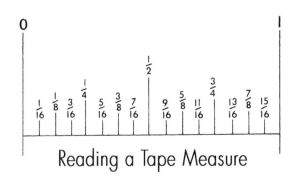

Reading a Tape Measure

Protecting Lumber from Decay

Moisture and warmth will promote decay of most woods. To prevent decay, naturally durable woods or preservative-treated wood must be used when the wood is exposed to moisture.

Decay resistant woods include Redwood, Cedar, Black Locust, and Black Walnut. Preservative-treated wood is treated according to certain industrial specifications. Preservative-treated wood is most commonly used because of its availability.

Preservative-treated or naturally durable woods should be used in the following locations:

1. On concrete foundation walls that are less than 8" from exposed earth. (Illustration D1)
2. On concrete or masonry slabs that are in direct contact with earth. (Illustration D2)
3. Where wood is attached directly to the interior of exterior masonry or concrete walls below grade. (Illustration D3)
4. Floor joists if they are closer than 18" to the exposed ground. (Illustration D4)
5. Floor girders if they are closer than 12" to the exposed ground. (Illustration D4)

Illustration D1

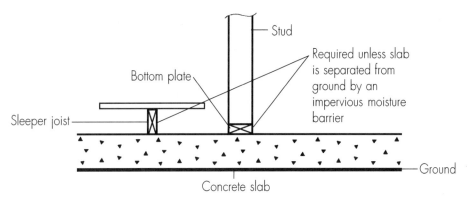

Stud

Bottom plate

Required unless slab
is separated from
ground by an
impervious moisture
barrier

Sleeper joist

Ground

Concrete slab

Illustration D2

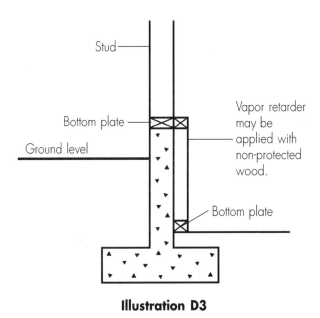

Stud

Bottom plate

Ground level

Vapor retarder
may be
applied with
non-protected
wood.

Bottom plate

Illustration D3

Joists

Girder

18" or less

12" or less

Ground

Illustration D4

17

Chapter Two

Nailing Patterns

Building codes and generally accepted practices were followed in developing these nailing patterns, which apply when the plans do not specify something different. When the plans call for other nailing patterns, be sure to follow them.

If you are framing every day, these patterns will soon become second nature. For the part-time framer, this chapter can serve as a quick reference.

You will notice in this chapter that there are different nails specified for the same nailing. There are four categories of nails: common nails, box nails, sinker nails, and gun nails. You will see a 3" × .131" nail specified frequently. This nail is the most common P-nail, or pneumatic gun nail, used.

The common nails are listed because they are typically specified in the code books. Most of the tests that are done to determine the strength needed use common nails. Box nails and sinker nails are listed because they are easier to nail, and less likely to split the wood. They are also commonly found at nail suppliers. The gun nails are listed because nail guns are used most.

Please note that common nails are listed with "common" written behind the size. If the nail size has "common" behind it, you can only use common nails. If it does not, you can use either common, box, or sinker nails.

Contents

Nail Top Plate to Studs

Two 16d common nails or three 3" x .131" nails through top plate into studs

Top plate

Stud

Two 16d common nails or three 3" x .131" nails

Top or bottom plate

Stud

Nail Bottom Plate to Studs

Stud

Bottom plate

Two 16d common nails or three 3" x .131" nails through bottom plate into studs

Alternate: Toenail four 8d common nails or four 3" x .131" nails

Nail Double Plate to Top Plate

One 16d nail or two 3" x .131" nails at 16" O.C. (on center). Stagger 16d nails.

Four 16d common nails or six 3" x .131" nails each side of splice in top and double plate.

Nail over studs to allow plumber's and electrician's drills to pass freely through the place between the studs.

Nail Corner

Nail Walls Together or Nail Double Studs

Five 16d common nails or seven 3" x .131" nails into studs. Start 6" from top and bottom.

16d common nails maximum spacing 24" O.C. or 3" x .131" nails maximum spacing 16" O.C.

Five 16d common nails or seven 3" x .131" nails into studs. Start 6" from top and bottom.

16d common nails maximum spacing 24" O.C. or 3" x .131" nails maximum spacing 16" O.C.

Nail Trimmer to Stud

4"

24"

24"

24"

6"

Two nails 4" from top of trimmer.

Stagger center nails.
16d common nails
maximum spacing 24" O.C.
nail at slight angle so that
the points of the nails
will not stick through.
3" x .131 nails
maximum spacing 16" O.C.

One nail approximately
6" from the bottom
centered.

Concrete Nailing

Bearing Walls

One 2½" concrete nail at 16" O.C.,
or at every stud.

When anchor bolts are used to
secure the bottom plate to the
concrete, concrete nails are only
needed between the anchor bolts
when necessary to straighten the
plate or secure the ends of the plate.

Nonbearing Walls

One 2½" concrete nail at 32" O.C.,
or at every other stud.

Nailing the Bearing and Nonbearing Walls to Floor Perpendicular to Joists

Stud

Bottom plate

Joists at 16" O.C. (on center)

Bearing Walls
Three 16d nails
or 3" x .131" nails
into each joist.
If wall sits on a rim joist
or blocking, place third nail
at center of joist space
and nail into rim or block.

Stud

Bottom plate

Joists at 16" O.C. (on center)

Subfloor
sheathing

Nonbearing Walls
One 16d nail
into each joist or
two 3" x .131" into
each joist.

Nailing the Bearing and Nonbearing Walls to Floor Parallel to Joists

Stud

Bottom plate

Joist

Braced wall panels nailed with same pattern as bearing walls.

Bearing Walls
Three 16d nails or 3" x .131" nails
per stud into each joist. If wall sits
on a rim joist or blocking, place
third nail at center of joist space
and nail into rim or block.

Subfloor
sheathing

Nonbearing Walls
One 16d nail
into each joist or
two 3" x .131" into
each joist.

Nail Header to Stud

4 x 8 or 6 x 8 Header

Four 16d nails or 3" x .131" nails

Trimmer

Studs

4 x 10 or 6 x 10 Header

Five 16d nails or 3" x .131" nails

Trimmer

Stud

4 x 12 or 6 x 12 Header

Six 16d nails or 3" x .131" nails

Trimmer

Stud

Headers made up of 2x lumber with ½" plywood sandwiches between should be nailed similarly.

L - Header

Three 16d nails or 3" x .131" nails

Trimmer

Stud

24

Nail Let-in Bracing

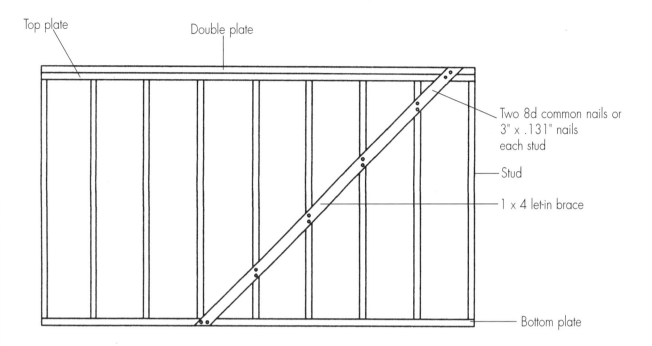

Top plate

Double plate

Two 8d common nails or
3" x .131" nails
each stud

Stud

1 x 4 let-in brace

Bottom plate

Two 8d nails at stud intersections
45 degree is best angle
Cross five studs if possible

Nail End of Joist

Three 16d common nails or
five 3" x .131" nails
through rim joist

Two 16d nails, or
3" or .131" nails
toenail.
One on each size of joists.

Nail Rim Joist

Rim joist

16d at 6" O.C. or
8d at 6" O.C. or
3" x .131" at 6" O.C.

Top plate

Double plate

Stud

Bottom plate

Nail Sheathing

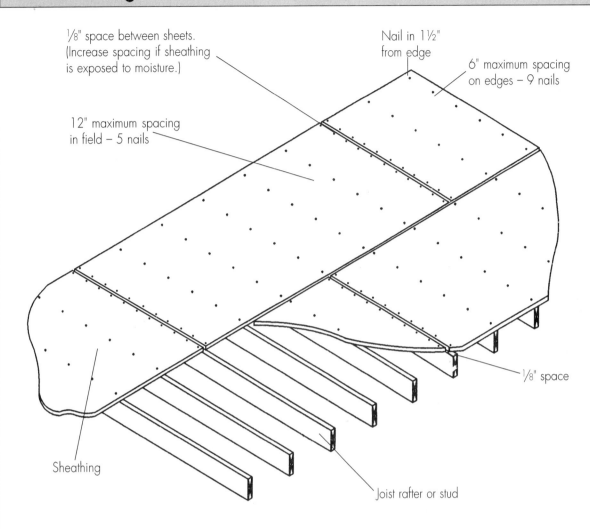

⅛" space between sheets. (Increase spacing if sheathing is exposed to moisture.)

Nail in 1½" from edge

6" maximum spacing on edges – 9 nails

12" maximum spacing in field – 5 nails

⅛" space

Sheathing

Joist rafter or stud

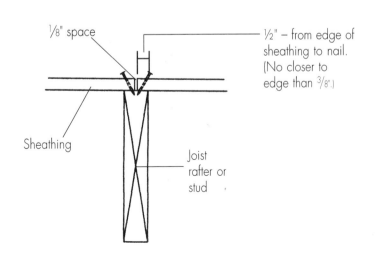

⅛" space

½" – from edge of sheathing to nail. (No closer to edge than ⅜".)

Sheathing

Joist rafter or stud

Nail size depends on sheathing thickness

½" or less
6d common nail or 2-½" × .131" nail

19/32" to ¾"
8d common nail or 2-½" × .131" nail

Nail Built-up Girders and Beams

24"   24"   24"

1"

1"

Three 16d nails of 3" × .131"
nails at ends and at
each splice

16d nails or 3" x .131" nail at
24" O.C. along top and bottom
staggered on each side of each layer

Nail Joist Blocking

Block

Double plate

Top plate

Stud

Joist

Six 16d nails or
3" x .131" nails or
8d common nails
2 – one side
1 – other side
3 – into double plate

Nail Lapping Joists

Two 16d or 3" x .131" nails on the end of each joist

Two 16d or 3" or .131" nails on the end of each joist

Two 16d or 3" x .131" nails, toenail outside of each joist into double plate

Nail Drywall Backing

16d nail at 16" O.C. over each stud

Rim joist

2 x 4 backing

Double plate

Top plate

Stud

Drywall

Drywall backing

Joist

Top plate

Double plate

Stud

Drywall

Nail Trusses to Wall

Three 16d nails or
3" x .131" nails
8d common nails.
Two on one side and
one on the other side.

Roof truss

Stud

Double plate

Top plate

Nail Ceiling Joist

Connecting rafter to ridge board
Two 16d common nails or
three 3" x .131" nails,
toenail or face nail.

Ridge board

Rafter

Ceiling joists

Double plate

Double plate

Connecting lapped ceiling
joists to each other and to wall
Connecting ceiling joists
Three 16d common nails or
four 3" x .131"
Ceiling joists to double plate
Three 16d nails or
three 3" x .131" nails or
three 8d common nails

Connecting ceiling joists to rafter to wall
Joint ceiling joists and rafters
Three 16d common nails or four 3" x .131" nails
Toenail from ceiling joists into double plate
Three 16d nails or three 3" x .131" nails or three 8d common nails
Toenail from rafter into double plate
Three 16d nails or 3" x .131" nails or 8d common nails

Nail Rafters to Wall

Rafter

Three 16d nails or 3" x .131" nails or
8d common nails.
Two one side and one the other side.

Double plate

Nail Blocks

Block position
depends on exterior
finish and venting

Block

Rafter

Four 16d nails or 3" x .131" nails,
two on each side of block.

Double plate

Top plate

Three 16d nails or 3" x .131 "
or 8d common nails.
Toenail from block into
double plate.

Stud

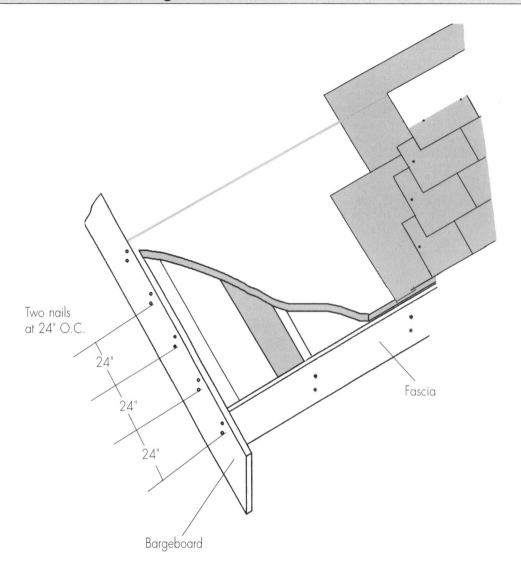

Two nails
at 24" O.C.

24"

24"

24"

Fascia

Bargeboard

- 1" fascia – use 8d galvanized box nails
- 2" fascia – use 16d galvanized box nails

Chapter Three

Floor Framing

This chapter illustrates the basic sequence for floor framing. Straight cuts and tight nailing make for a neat and professional job. Pay particular attention to the corners. It is important that they stay square and plumb up from the walls below, so the building does not gain or lose in size. Also pay close attention to laying the first sheet of subfloor sheathing. If it is laid straight and square, the entire subfloor will go down easily and require no unnecessary cuts. If you make a sloppy start on the first sheet, you'll struggle to make each sheet fit, you'll waste valuable time, and you won't be proud of the results.

Contents

Steps:

Look for crown

Top

Crown up

Mark joist

Joist

Double plate

Stud

Spread joists so crowns are in the same direction.

The crown is the highest point of a curved piece of lumber.

If the joists are sitting on a foundation instead of a stud wall, then a sill plate, or mudsill would be attached to the foundation, and the joists would sit on the plate or sill.

Double plate

Rim joist

Stud

Joist

Cut line:
Chalk line 1½" in on joist from outside of wall.
This space allows for the rim joist.

If joists lap over an interior wall, they can be rough-cut approximately two inches beyond the wall. Do not let lapped joists go more than six inches beyond the wall.

Two 16d or 3" x .131" nails.
Toenail from each joist into double plate.
One on each side.

Rim joist

Three 16d common nails or
five 3" x .131" nails
into each joist.

Joist

Stud

Double plate

Turn joists crown up and nail into place.

Trimmer joist
Double if header joist is more than
4' long or if header joist is more than
3' from trimmer joist bearing.

Tail joist
If 12' or longer, support with
framing anchors or hangers.

Header joist
Double if longer than 4'.
If longer than 6', support with
framing anchors or hangers.

Tail joist

Rim joist

Trimmer joist

Five 16d nails or
3" x .131" nails

Header joist

Tail joist

Joist

Nail joists to walls to hold interior walls in place.

Block

One 16d nail per joist

Rim joist

Rim joist

Double plate

Top plate

Studs

Cutting Blocks

16" O.C. spacing
  Single joist blocks — $14^{7}/_{16}$"
  Lapped joist blocks — $12^{7}/_{8}$"

24" O.C. spacing
  Single joist blocks — $22^{7}/_{16}$"
  Lapped joist blocks — $20^{7}/_{8}$"

Subfloor sheathing

Drywall backing

Nail one 16d nail over each stud and at ends.

Joist

Double plate

Top plate

Stud

Whenever the distance from the edge of the wall to the joist is greater than 6", place drywall backing on top of the wall.

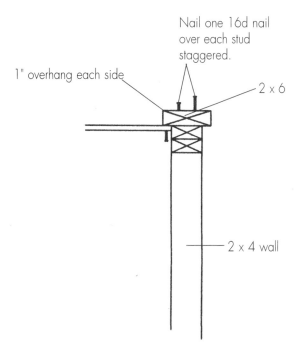

Nail one 16d nail over each stud staggered.

1" overhang each side

2 x 6

2 x 4 wall

Start second row with half sheet so ends will be staggered.

1. Chalk a line at 4'-¼" on joists.

6. Nail remaining joists, setting them to layout marks.

1/8" gap – larger if moist application (check with instructions on sheathing)

5. Nail on chalk line and layout mark.

2. Apply glue to joists, if called for.

4. Pull layout on sheathing.

3. Nail on chalk line along center of joist.

Six Steps for Setting First Sheet of Sheathing

1. Chalk a line 4'-¼" in from one rim to its opposite, perpendicular to the joists.
2. Apply glue to joists, if called for. Be sure to nail sheathing before glue dries.
3. Center first piece of sheathing to last joist on the chalk line and nail each end.
4. Pull joist layout from corner of sheathing and mark sheathing.
5. Nail sheathing to joist next to rim joist along chalk line and layout mark.
6. Set remaining joists to layout marks and nail.

Setting Second Sheet

Set to chalk line and layout mark.

Setting Second Row and Remaining Sheets

Set to existing sheets allowing ⅛" gaps.

Stagger sheet ends on joists.

Make sure rim joists are straight before they are nailed.

Chapter Four

Wall Framing

There are many ways to frame walls, but it is always good to follow an organized sequence. This **sixteen-step sequence** has been developed over years of framing. Following these steps will help you and your crew work efficiently and eliminate errors. It will also ensure consistency from framer to framer. For example, if you have to leave a wall in the middle of framing it to go to another task, another framer can easily pick up where you left off and proceed without having to check every nail to see what you have done.

Keep in mind, walls must be *square, plumb,* and *level.* Measure accurately, cut straight, and nail tight.

Contents

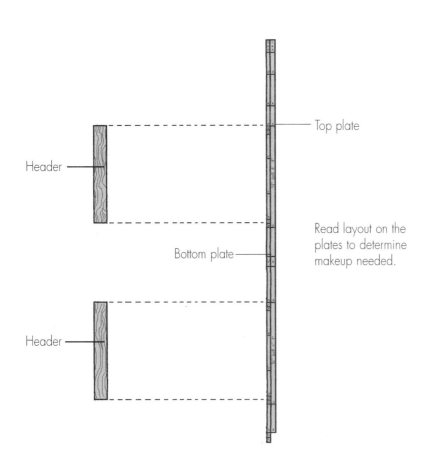

Header

Top plate

Header

Bottom plate

Read layout on the
plates to determine
makeup needed.

Corner

Cripple

Header

Sill

Bottom plate

Backer

Top plate

Trimmer

Stud

Header

Sill

Cripple

Beam pocket

W3-Spread Studs
W4-Nail Headers to Studs
W5-Nail Top Plate to Studs and Headers
W6-Nail Bottom Plate to Studs
W7-Nail Double Plate to Studs

Corner

Top plate

Stud trimmer

Cripples

Sill

Backer

Double plate

Bottom plate

Header

Beam pocket

Exterior Wall

16d nails every 4 to 8 ft. to hold bottom plate straight to chalk line.

Chalk line

Exterior of building

Bottom plate

After squaring wall, toenail two 16d nails through double plate into floor.

Toenail bottom plate to chalk line.

To square a wall, secure the bottom plate as shown, then move the top of the wall until the diagonal dimensions are equal. Once the wall is square, secure it with two nails through the double plate into the floor.

Nail on the inside of the bottom plate so the nails will hold the wall in position while it is being stood.

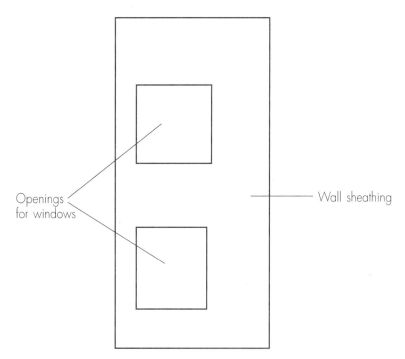

Openings for windows

Wall sheathing

Cover the entire wall with sheathing, then rout window and door openings with a panel pilot router bit. Save the leftover pieces of sheathing for small areas and filling in between floors.

If the first floor exterior walls can be reached from the ground, then the sheathing is not installed until after the walls are plumb and lined. This eliminates the potential problem of a square wall sitting on a foundation that is not level.

W10-Installing Nail-Flange Windows in Wall Before Wall is Stood Up

a. Check plans for correct window.

b. Check window opening for protrusions (nails, wood splinters, etc.) that might hold window away from edge.

c. Install window flashing (see "Window Flashing Installation" Chapter 6)

d. Set window in opening, making sure window is right side up.

e. Slide window to each end of opening and draw a line on the sheathing with a pencil along the edge of window (draw lines before caulking window).

f. Center window in marks you have just drawn.

g. Nail window sides and bottoms, using appropriate nails.

1st 2nd 3rd

4th 5th

Thick lines are pencil marks.

Thin line is window.

Dotted line is rough opening.

W11-Stand Wall
W12-Set Bottom Plate
W13-Set Double Plate
W14-Set Reveal
W15-Nail Wall

W14

Nail the end stud to set the reveal* in the middle of the wall where the two walls join. The reveal in the middle of the wall should be the same as the top and bottom reveal.

* The reveal is the amount of space on the corner stud of a wall after another wall is joined to it.

W13

Set double plate.
Make sure top plates are down tight to studs.

W15

Nail walls together and nail bottom plate.

W12

Set bottom plates to chalk lines.

Double plate

Top plate

Stud

Bottom plate

W16-Plumb and Line

"Plumb and line" is the process of making the walls straight and true.

"Plumbing" is the use of a level to set the ends of the walls plumb or perfectly upright.

"Lining" is using a tight string attached to the top of a wall to use as a guide for straightening it.

String Line

Nail

Set 16d nail in corner of double plate and bend until it is in line with wall below.

Set nails at either end of wall as shown, and then string line tightly between them, adjusting the line so that it is about ½" above the double plate. Wall should be moved in or out to align with string.

The walls are braced with 2 × 4 lumber to hold them and, if necessary, make them plumb and straight.

If a wall already is sheathed and in place, but not plumb, correct it if it is more than ¼" out of plumb for standard height walls.

Pulling Brace

Temporary brace

Nail when wall is straight.

Push until wall is straight.

Push-brace

Blocks to hold brace

Double plate

Top plate

Wall

Bottom plate

Toenail push-brace

Racking Brace

Do not let brace protrude above double plate.

Two 16d nails in top plate.

One 16d nail in center if it is a bearing wall, exterior wall, or will be used for walking up.

Use crowbar to rack brace and wall. Turn brace around if wall needs to be racked in other direction.

Two 16d nails into bottom plate.

Chapter Five

Roof Framing

Framing a roof is the most difficult aspect of the trade, and the ability to construct a roof is a real test of your framing skills. Planning a roof requires knowledge of some rather complicated geometry, and building it means working in often awkward positions, at heights, with long and heavy pieces of lumber. The hardest part is calculating the lengths and angles for cutting rafters. Don't expect to be able to read this chapter and go out and frame a roof. Being able to frame a roof takes time, experience, and many wrong cuts. Don't get discouraged by mistakes and setbacks on the first few roofs you do. Knowledge comes from struggling through failure: learn from your mistakes.

This manual presents four methods for finding the rafter length. The first is the "Pythagorean Theorem." To use this method you need to have a basic knowledge of geometry and access to a calculator with a square root key. A framing square with a rafter table imprinted on it is required for both the "Framing Square Rafter Table" method and the "Framing Square Stepping" method. Possibly the easiest method is the "Chalking Lines Duplication" method.

Construction calculators, available at most construction supply stores, can make the process of finding the rafter lengths a lot easier. Typically they

Contents

have a run and rise button for entering those dimensions and a diagonal button to calculate what would be the rafter length. These calculators also calculate in feet and inches, which makes figuring a lot easier. If you have much roof framing to do, these calculators are definitely a good investment.

Prefabricated trusses, factory-made from the architect's specifications, require, of course, no calculations on your part; and being uniform in size, are somewhat easier to work with than ridgeboards and rafters. Still, they are heavy and you are working at heights. You must be constantly aware of what you and the other two crew members are doing. Planning and teamwork are required. Before you have the trusses set on the roof, make sure you spend some time thinking about the easiest way for them to go up. If they get set on the roof in a disorganized manner, it can mean much extra work and a lot of aggravation moving them around on top of the walls.

Roof Framing Terms

Ridge

Common rafter

Valley jack rafter

Ridge

Common rafter

Hip jack rafter

Valley rafter

Hip rafter

Bird's-mouth

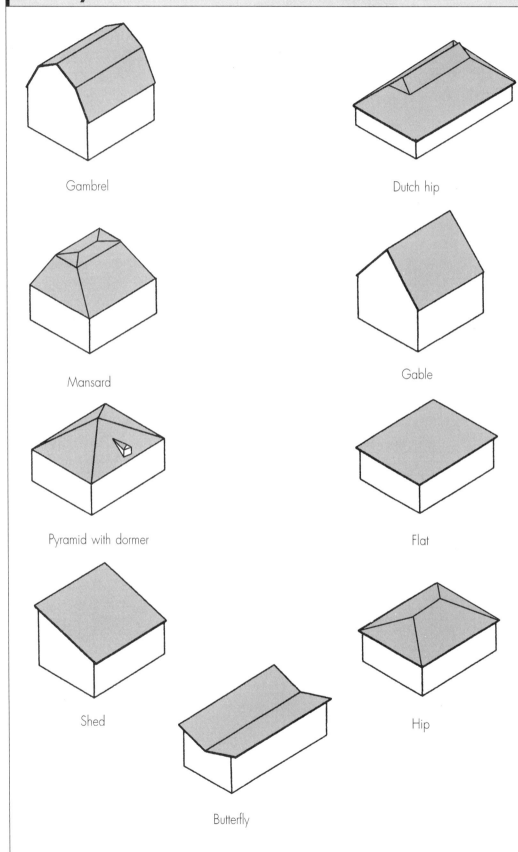

Gambrel

Dutch hip

Mansard

Gable

Pyramid with dormer

Flat

Shed

Hip

Butterfly

R1-Finding the Lengths of Common Rafters

There are four methods for finding common rafter lengths. Study them all and use the one that works best for you.

A. Pythagorean Theorem

B. Framing-Square Rafter Table

C. Framing-Square Stepping Method

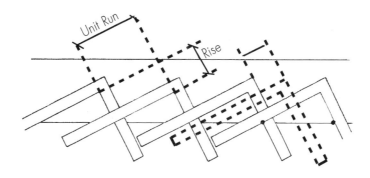

D. Chalking Lines Duplication Method

Pythagoras was an ancient Greek philosopher and mathematician. His famous theorem states that the square of the hypotenuse of a right triangle is equal to the sum of the squares of the two other sides. Thus:

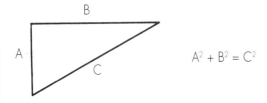

$$A^2 + B^2 = C^2$$

In roof framing, A = the Rise, B = the Run, and C (the hypotenuse) = the Rafter Length.

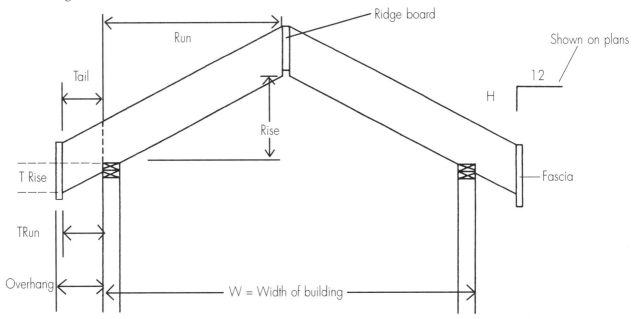

Run = ½ building width – ½ ridge board width
H = is given on plans = the amount of rise per foot of run

Rafter Cut Length = Rafter Length + Rafter Tail Length

Finding Rafter Length

First, find the run by using the following formula:
Run = ½ building width – ½ ridge board width

Second, find the rise by using the following formula:
Rise = H/12 × Run

Third, find the Rafter Length by using the following formula:
Rafter Length = $\sqrt{(\text{Rise} \times \text{Rise}) + (\text{Run} \times \text{Run})}$

To apply this formula, multiply Rise × Rise, and then Run × Run. Add the two sums, then press the square root key on your calculator. The result is the Rafter Length.

Finding Rafter Tail (T) Length

First, find the TRun by using the following formula:

TRun = Overhang – Fascia

Second, find the TRise using the following formula:

TRise = H/12 × TRun

Third, find the Rafter Tail Length by using the following formula:

Rafter Tail Length = $\sqrt{(TRise \times TRise) + (TRun \times TRun)}$

Note: Be sure to mark crowns on rafters prior to measuring and cutting. Crowns are always up.

Example: Finding Rafter Cut Length

Rafter Length:

Let the pitch be $4\overline{\smash{\big)}12}$ and the building width be 20' and the ridge board be 1½" thick.

Step 1: Run = ½ (20') – ½ (1½") = 9'-11¼"

Step 2: Rise = $^4/_{12}$ × 9'-11¼"

= .3333 × 119.25"

= 39.75

= 39¾"

Step 3: Rafter Length = $\sqrt{(119.25 \times 119.25) + (39.75 \times 39.75)}$

= $\sqrt{14{,}220.56 + 1{,}580.06}$

= $\sqrt{15{,}800.62}$

= 125.70

= 125$^{11}/_{16}$"

Rafter Tail Length:

Let overhang be 2' and fascia be 1½".

Step 1: TRun = 2' – 1½" = 1'-10½"

Step 2: TRise = $^4/_{12}$ × 1'-10½"

= .3333 × 22.5" = 7.49

= 7.49

= 7½"

Step 3: Rafter Tail Length = $\sqrt{(7.49 \times 7.49) + (22.5 \times 22.5)}$

= $\sqrt{56.10 + 506.25}$

= $\sqrt{562.35}$

= 23.71

= 23$^{11}/_{16}$"

Rafter Cut Length = 125$^{11}/_{16}$ + 23$^{11}/_{16}$

= 149$^3/_8$"

B-Framing-Square Rafter Table

Steps

1. Find pitch of roof from plans.
2. Find pitch on framing-square inch line.
3. Find multiplication factor below pitch number.
4. Find run of rafter and multiply by multiplication factor.
5. Subtract ½ thickness of ridge board to determine the rafter length.

Example

Let the pitch be 4$\overline{|}$12 and the run be 10'.

Step 1 = 4
Step 2 = 4
Step 3 = 12.65
Step 4 = 10 × 12.65 = 126.5"
Step 5 = 126.5" − ¾" = 125.75" rafter length

Rafter Tail Length for overhang is found using the same method as for the rafter length except that Step 5 (subtraction for ridge board) is eliminated. The rafter tail length is then added on to the rafter length to produce the rafter tail cut length.

C-Framing-Square Stepping Method

The pitch of the roof is given on the plans in this way: $6\lceil^{12}$

The number 12 is constant and indicates 12 inches of run, or horizontal distance. The other number represents the rise and varies, depending on how steep the roof is. The example below indicates that for every 12" of run, or horizontal distance, there is 6" of rise, or vertical distance. The greater this number, the steeper the roof.

To find the rafter length, first lay the framing square on the rafter at 12" on the blade and the amount of rise on the tongue. Once the framing square is set with stair nuts, just step off the amount of run along the rafter.

Example
Let the run equal 10'-4"
Let the overhang equal 1'-6"

1. Set framing square with stair nuts: the run, 12", on the blade; the rise, 6", on the tongue.

2. Step off 11'.

3. Perpendicular to the end lines mark 4" (top), and 6" (bottom). Place the square at those marks to draw the plumb lines for the ridge and tail cuts.

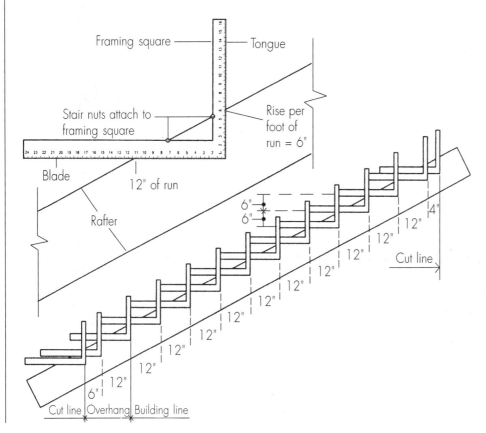

This method is probably the easiest to use. To find the lengths of rafters you make an actual size drawing of the rafter on the floor and then measure the length.

All the information you need to use this method should be on the plans. First you will need the *pitch* (see Method C on the previous page). Second is the *span,* which is the distance from the support on one side of the rafter to the support on the other side. Third is the *width* of the rafter, the length of the roof overhang, and the size of the exterior wall.

Steps:

1. Chalk a straight line longer than the length of your rafter, which would represent the bottom of the ceiling joist if there were a ceiling joist.
2. Chalk two lines perpendicular to the first line to represent the exterior wall.
3. From the point where your inside exterior wall line crosses the ceiling joist line, measure out and up according to your pitch $\times \frac{12}{\Gamma}$. For this example let your pitch equal $6\frac{12}{\Gamma}$. Therefore for every 12" you measure out, you measure 6" up. The longer the distance out, the greater your accuracy. Make sure that the line up is exactly perpendicular or square. You can use surrounding walls that are square to measure from or measure a 3-4-5 triangle.
4. Chalk a line for the thickness of the rafter.
5. Measure the distance for the span along the ceiling joists line, then make a perpendicular line up and mark the ridge board.
6. Measure the distance of the roof overhang and draw in the fascia board.

With these lines in place you can measure all the lengths you will need to cut your rafters.

R2-Cut Common Rafter

A. Rafter cut length
B. Bird's-mouth
C. Angle cuts

A. Rafter Cut Length

Rafter length
(see previous section).

Length of overhang
(find in same manner as rafter).

Mark and make
ridge cut.

See cutting
bird's-mouth
next page.

Building line

Mark tail cut
same as ridge cut.

Set speed square to H (which is given on plans).
H = the amount of rise per foot of run.
This speed square, as an example, is set to H = 4.

Shown on plans like this: $4\overline{|}^{12}$ Usually shown on elevation sheet above the roof.

Cut a pattern first and try it for fit before cutting all the rafters. A framing square can also be used to mark cut lines (see illustration in "Framing-Square Stepping Method").

B. Bird's-Mouth

Steps:
1. Mark rafter length.
2. Mark building line at rafter length for the correct pitch.
3. Mark parallel plumb line a distance equal to width of wall and toward interior of building.
4. Mark seat cut square (90°) from building line at rafter length and bottom of parallel line.
5. Cut bird's-mouth.

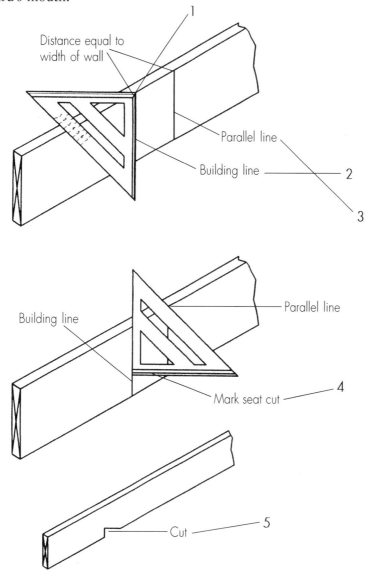

A framing square can also be used to mark a bird's-mouth. (See illustration in "Framing-Square Stepping Method.")

C. Angle Cuts

Set saw at 90° and cut,
after using the Common scale
on the speed square to mark the rafter.

Set saw at 45° and cut,
after using the Common scale
on the speed square to mark the rafter.

Set saw at 45° and cut,
after using the Common scale
on speed square to mark the rafter.

Set saw at 45° and cut,
after using the Hip-Val scale
on speed square
to mark the rafter.

Set saw at 90° and cut,
after using the Common scale
on the speed square to mark the rafter.

Use numbers on speed square to match pitch on roof.

Hip-Val scale

Common scale

Height of Temporary Ridge Board Support

Height of temporary ridge support =
Rise + length of plumb from bird's-mouth seat cut
    – width of ceiling joist
    – thickness of temporary sheathing
    – ridge board width

Nail two 16d common nails or three 3" x .131" nails through ridge board into rafter. Toenail when necessary.

Common rafter

Ridge board

Common rafter

Temporary ridge support

Top plate

Temporary sheathing

Ceiling joist

Studs

Double plate

To start the ridge board layout, plumb a line up from a string held tight between roof layout marks on opposite walls. From that point, mark the ridge board layout to match the roof layout on the double plate.

Begin by setting the end rafters, as shown. Set the remaining rafters in the order that works best for you. As in lining a wall, attach a string in a similar manner along the edge of the ridge board. This will guide you in keeping a straight ridge board while you set the remaining rafters.

R5-Length of Hip and Valley Rafters

The length of the hip and valley rafters can be found by using any of the four common rafter methods previously described, and then making adjustments for the run and the top and bottom cuts.

Adjustment for the Run

For every 12" of common rafter run, there is 16.97" (17" approx.) of run for hip and valley rafters.

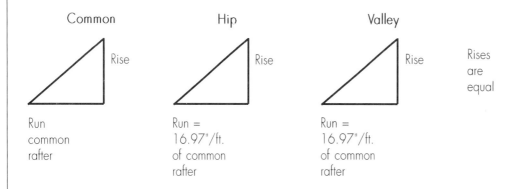

Multiply the run in feet of the common rafter by 16.97" (17 is commonly used) to get the run of the hip or valley rafter.

Adjustments for the Top and Bottom Cuts

The cut mark will be made similar to the common rafter cut mark, except that the hip-val scale on the speed square will be used instead of the common scale to mark the line to cut. (See "Rafter Cut Length" and "Angle Cuts.")

If a framing square is used, use the same procedure shown previously, except use 17 instead of 12 along the blade of the framing square.

These procedures assume a hip or valley corner of 90 degrees.

Bottom Adjustment

Top Adjustment

Hip Rafter Length (HRL) = Hip rafter length before adjustments (HRBA) – ½ diagonal thickness (DT) of rafter – thickness (T) of rafter (½ thickness top and bottom combined)

or

HRL = HRBA – ½ DT – T

These figures are based on a 90-degree building corner.

Valley rafter length before adjustment (VRBA) (see "Length of")

Valley rafter length (VRL)

Bottom Adjustment

Top Adjustment

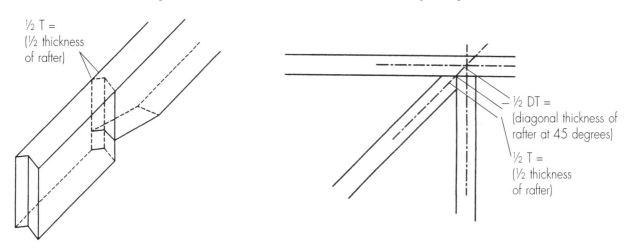

½ T = (½ thickness of rafter)

½ DT = (diagonal thickness of rafter at 45 degrees)

½ T = (½ thickness of rafter)

Valley Rafter Length = Valley rafter length before adjustment − ½ diagonal thickness of rafter. (The ½ thickness factors cancel each other out.)

or

VRL = VRBA − ½ DT

These figures are based on a 90-degree building corner.

Set Hip Rafters

Four 16d nails, or
3" × .131 nails
two each from
adjoining rafters

Three 8d nails, 16d
nails, or 3" × .131
nails, 2 in one side,
one in opposite side of
rafter into double plate

Set Valley Rafters

Four 16d nails or
3" × .131 nails,
two each from
adjoining rafters

Three 8d nails, 16d
nails, or 3" × .131
nails, 2 in one side,
one in opposite rafter
into double plate

Note: If hip or valley rafters do not fit, first check your length calculations,
   then check walls for plumb and the ridge board for correct height and for plumb.

Set first jack rafter on 16" or 24" spacing with common rafters.

Measure length from common rafter to first jack rafter and then use standard jack rafter differences, as given in framing square table, to measure lengths of remaining jack rafters along the hip rafter.

Framing Square Table

LENGTH	COMMON	RAFTERS	PER FOOT	RUN	21 63	20 81	20
"	HIP OR	VALLEY	" "	"	24 74	24 02	23 32
DIFF	IN LENGTH	OF JACKS	16 INCHES	CENTERS	28 7/8	27 3/4	26 11/16
"	"	"	2 FEET	"	43 1/4	41 5/8	40
SIDE	CUT	OF	JACKS	USE	6 11/16	6 15/16	7 3/16
"	"	HIP OR	VALLEY	"	8 1/4	8 1/2	8 3/4

Rafter

Ridge board

Two 16d nails
through rafter
into lookout

Subfascia

Two 16d nails
through subfascia
into lookout
let in to rafter

Two galvanized
box nails, 24" O.C.
through fascia into subfascia

For 1" fascia, use 8d nails.
For 2" fascia, use 16d nails.

Fascia

If overhang is exposed underneath, use ccx plywood for exposed portion.

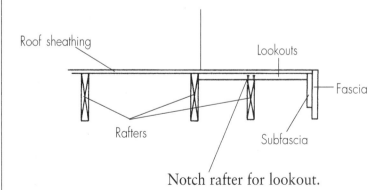

Roof sheathing

Lookouts

Fascia

Rafters

Subfascia

Notch rafter for lookout.

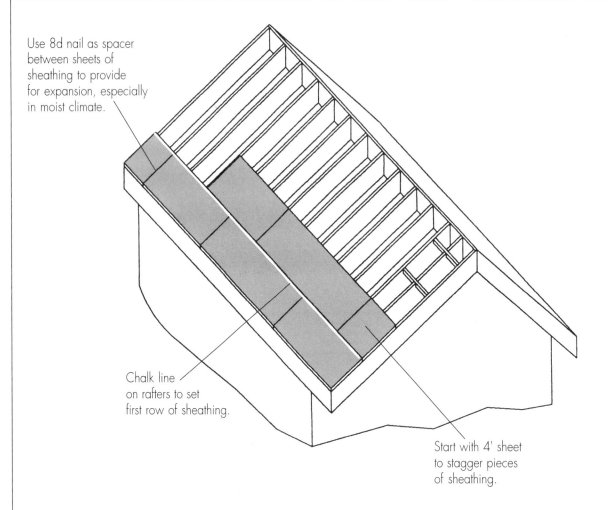

Use 8d nail as spacer between sheets of sheathing to provide for expansion, especially in moist climate.

Chalk line on rafters to set first row of sheathing.

Start with 4' sheet to stagger pieces of sheathing.

Cover Fascia

Hide Sheathing

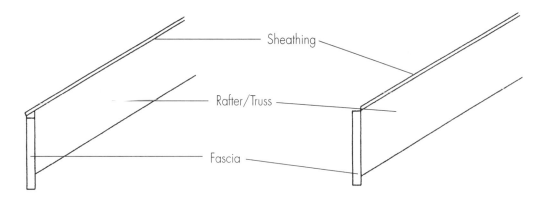

Sheathing

Rafter/Truss

Fascia

Sheathing covers fascia.

Fascia hides sheathing edge. Fascia is attached so that its top outer edge is in line with the plane of the top surface of the roof sheathing.

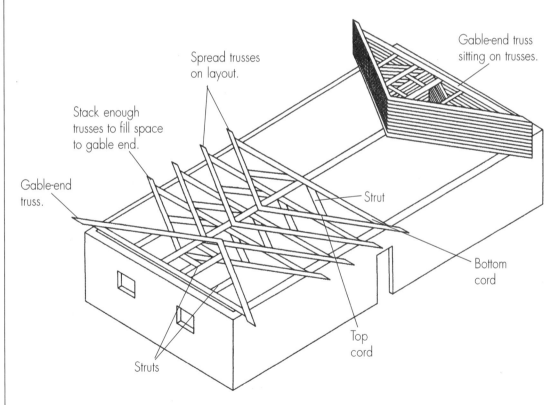

Spread trusses on layout.

Gable-end truss sitting on trusses.

Stack enough trusses to fill space to gable end.

Gable-end truss.

Strut

Bottom cord

Top cord

Struts

When trusses are delivered in stacks, they should be set on the roof to allow for easy spreading. The gable ends should be on top because they go up first. The direction of the ridge is important so they can be spread and tilted up easily.

T2-Sheath Gable Ends

When sheathing gable-end truss, check plans to see if a vent opening is shown.

- Set gable end in place.
- Center gable end on wall.
- Toenail through bottom of truss into plate so gable end is on chalk line 1½" in from outer edge of double plate.

T3-Set Gable Ends

Toenail 16d nails 24" O.C. to hold gable end while setting gable-end truss.

1½" chalk line

Truss

Wall

Temporary braces

Temporary braces

String line

Temporary spacer support

Temporary brace to interior wall

Steps

1. String line from center of gable ends.
2. Lift single truss into place.
3. Center truss on string line.
4. Nail truss to exterior wall on layout.
5. Nail through temporary spacer support near ridge of truss and on layout marked on temporary spacer support.
6. Set six trusses. Then check gable end for plumb and put permanent brace on gable end. Permanent brace should connect top of gable end to an interior wall or a cross support running between the trusses.
7. Every eight trusses, put an additional brace on trusses. Refer to truss specifications for additional braces.

Ceiling joists serve two basic functions: they provide support for the ceiling sheathing and the support needed to keep the rafters from pushing the walls out.

Rafters that are not supported at the top or somewhere along the span by a beam, create an outward force on the wall they rest on. This force is frequently offset by ceiling joists joining the walls on the opposite side of the roof.

The chart below shows a common size of ceiling joist needed for different spans.

Species & Grade	Maximum Ceiling Joist Spans		
	2 × 4	2 × 6	2 × 8
Douglas Fir-Larch # 1	7'-8"	11'-2"	14'-2"
Douglas Fir-Larch # 2	7'-2"	10'-6"	13'-3"
Douglas Fir-Larch # 3	5'-5"	7'-11"	10'-0"
Hem-Fir # 1	7'-6"	10'-11"	13'-10"
Hem-Fir # 2	7'-1"	10'-4"	13'-1"
Hem-Fir # 3	5'-5"	7'-11"	10'-0"
Southern Pine # 1	8'-0"	12'-6"	15'-10"
Southern Pine # 2	7'-8"	11'-0"	14'-2"
Southern Pine # 3	5'-9"	8'-6"	10'-10"
Spruce-Pine-Fir # 1	7'-2"	10'-6"	13'-3"
Spruce-Pine-Fir # 2	7'-2"	10'-6"	13'-3"
Spruce-Pine-Fir # 3	5'-5"	7'-11"	10'-0"

The bottom cord of roof trusses acts as a ceiling joist and provides support for the ceiling sheathing, and support to keep the walls from pushing out.

Attic areas above ceiling joists must be made accessible if there is a clear height of 30" or more. This requires framing an attic opening. The opening must not be less than 20" by 30" and have at least 30" clear space above. The attic access should be framed similar to an opening in floor joists as illustrated on F5-Frame Openings in Joists in Chapter 3.

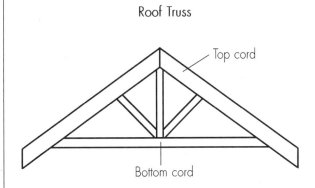

Roof Truss

Top cord

Bottom cord

Rafters

Ceiling joist

The block trusses, lookouts, fascia, and sheathing installations described in
the previous pages are shown below, in actual project photos.

T5 - Block trusses   T5 - Block trusses   T7 - Fascia

T6 - Lookouts
T8 - Sheathing

Chapter Six

Doors, Windows, and Stairs

D oors and windows are two of the few finish items that framers handle. It is important that time and care are taken to ensure they are installed in a proper, professional manner. Put your framing hammer in the tool box and use, instead, a lighter, smoother-faced trim hammer and a nail set.

Exterior, prehung doors are the type covered in this chapter. They are the ones framers most commonly work with, and most of the skills involved in hanging them will carry over to the hanging of interior doors. The first door you hang on any job will give you the most difficulty. If you have more than one door to hang, do them one after the other; each door will go in a little easier than the one before.

Nail-flange windows and sliding glass doors will vary depending on the manufacturer. You will find here the basic principles of their installation. Use common sense and follow the directions provided, and you should have little trouble installing these units.

Stairs represent one of the more difficult challenges to a framer's skill. As in roof framing, the geometry is a bit complicated, but taken step-by-step, the logic soon becomes clear, leading to successful execution of the plans. There are many different stair designs. The stair layout described in this chapter is typical. Be aware that the dimensions given on the plans do not always allow for enough headroom. Always check headroom and other dimensions by taking accurate on-site measurements.

Contents

A calculator is handy, some might say necessary, for finding the rise and tread dimensions when not given on the plans. Always double- or triple-check your calculations. Remember: measure twice, cut once. The finish floors at the top and bottom of stairs are often different. When cutting stair stringers, don't forget to check the plans for such differences and then check the height of your top and bottom risers to allow for them.

Door Framing Terms

Header jamb | Header | Double plate
Space for shimming
Top plate
Latch jamb
Door
Stud
Trimmer
Door hinge
Door stop and ⅛" gap
Stud
Hinge jamb
Shims
Threshold
Bottom plate

Steps for Installation of Exterior Prehung Doors

Steps

1. Read instructions that come with door.
2. Check plans for direction of door swing.
3. Check threshold for level (shim under hinge jamb if necessary).
4. Nail hinge jamb (do not set nails), and plumb both directions. Shim behind jamb if necessary to obtain plumb or if door needs to be centered.
5. Nail latch jamb using shims. Set so there is ⅛" margin between door and jamb and so top and bottom of door hit door stop at the same time when closing. Lock set holes also must line up.
6. Check door for total fit.
7. Nail door with six 16d galvanized casing nails in hinge jamb, two at each hinge, and four in latch jamb (one each at the top and bottom and two in the middle). This includes nails used in Steps 4 and 5.
8. Set nails and break or cut shims.
9. Check again for total fit.

1. READ INSTRUCTIONS
Usually there are instructions that come with the door. Check the instructions over for anything you might need to know.

2. CHECK PLANS
Check the building plans to find the direction of the door swing.

3. CHECK THE THRESHOLD
Check the threshold for level. Shim under hinge jamb if necessary.

One 16d galvanized casing nail at each hinge.
DO NOT SET NAILS

Shim under hinge jamb if floor is low.

4. NAIL HINGE JAMB
Nail hinge jamb tight to trimmer with one 16d galvanized casing nail at each hinge. Do not set nails. Plumb both directions. Shim behind jamb if necessary to obtain plumb or if door needs to be centered in opening.

One 16d galvanized casing nail at each hinge.
DO NOT SET NAILS

Pull casing in tight to wall.

5. NAIL LATCH JAMB

Before nailing the latch jamb, make sure of the following
three items:
1. Continuous gap between door and jamb is ⅛".
2. Door touches latch jamb equally at top and bottom.
3. The lockset hole in door and in the latch jamb line up.

Use two shims (three places) running opposite directions
so door jamb remains square. Shingles are commonly used for shims.

6. CHECK DOOR

Check door for total fit:
1. Gap around door is even.
2. Door and latch jamb align.
3. Door closes smoothly, no binding.
4. Lockset holes line up.
5. Door closes tight, no rattle.

7. NAIL DOOR

Six – 16d galvanized casing nails in hinge jamb — two at each hinge.
Four – 16d galvanized casing nails in latch jamb — one each top and bottom
and two near latch. This includes nails used in Steps 4 and 5.

8. SET NAILS AND TRIM SHIMS

9. FINAL CHECK

Check again for total fit (see Step 6).

Installation of Nail-Flange Window after Wall is Up

1. Install window flashing (see next page).
2. Set in place (from inside if possible).
3. Place temporary shims under bottom of window. Equalize space at top and bottom of window. Shims are usually $\frac{1}{8}$" to $\frac{1}{4}$".
4. Make gaps the same between window frame and trimmer on each side.
5. Nail top corners from outside.
6. Nail one bottom corner. (Do not set all the way.)
7. Place window slider in and check to see if the gap between the window slider and window frame is the same from top to bottom.
8. Check. If the gap is not equal, check both the rough opening and the window for square and adjust accordingly.
9. Finish nailing. Make sure gap is equal top, bottom, and middle. (Do not nail top of the window.)

View From Inside

Header

Minimum nailing:
Two nails on each side
and one in the bottom.
Increase the number of nails for
larger windows.
Use 8d nails.

Temporary shims

Stud

3. Apply a continuous seal (caulking) to the back side of the window flange near the outer edge to the outside of the window opening, at a point that ensures contact with the back side of the window flange. If window flange has nail slots, it is best to align seal with holes.

Header flashing needs to be applied when weather-resistant barrier (house wrap) and siding are applied.

2. Attach 9" wide flashing at each jamb. Start flashing 8½" above rough opening at header. Extend below over flashing at sill. Do not attach where it extends over sill flashing.

1. Attach 9" wide sill flashing. Fasten next to window rough opening. Extend 10" beyond rough opening. Do not attach ends or bottom. Prior to installation of the siding, weather-resistant barrier will be slid up under the flashing.

Flashing is attached easily with a staple hammer.

Steps for Installation of Sliding Glass Doors

1. **INSTRUCTIONS**
   Read and follow carefully the instructions that come with the door. Never assume what you do not know.

2. **SEAL THRESHOLD**
   Use neoprene or similar sealing compound to seal the threshold.

3. **INSTALL FLASHING**
   The jamb flashing with sealer is installed using a method similar to the jamb flashing on windows.

4. **PLACE DOOR**
   Place the door in position.

5. **CENTER TOP**
   Center the top of the door in rough opening.

6. **NAIL TOP CORNERS**
   Nail each corner of the top of the door through nail flange (do not set nails).

7. **ADJUST DOOR**
   Adjust the door frame so that the space between the door frame and wall trimmers is equal. Check for plumb with a level and adjust if necessary.

8. **COMPLETE NAILING**
   Close the door and latch it. Then nail off the sides using four 8d nails on each side. Do not nail top of door.

9. **ADJUST DOOR**
   Adjust the slider part of the door if necessary. Usually there is an adjustment screw at the bottom of the door. Tighten this screw to close a gap between the door and the jamb at the top of the door, or loosen to increase the gap.

10. **SCREWS**
    If screws come with the door, shim and tighten screws in the sides and bottom. Use predrilled holes.

Installation of Sliding Glass Doors

Sliding Glass Door — from Inside

5. Center top.

7. Adjust door for equal spaces.

2. Seal threshold.

Sliding Glass Door — from Outside

6. Nail top corners.

7. Adjust door.

9"

8 ½"

3. Install flashing; jamb flashing with sealer.

8. Complete nailing: four 8d nails each side.

2. Seal threshold.

Stair Installation

The three main dimensions in stair building are those for risers, treads, and headroom. The riser height and the tread width are usually given on the plans. You can generally use the tread width given on the plans. The riser height, however, is often not accurate enough to use.

Stair Installation Steps

1. **MEASURE HEIGHT**

   Measure the height of the stairwell from finish floor to finish floor.

2. **FIND RISER HEIGHT**

   Divide the height of the stairwell by the number of risers shown on the plan to determine the riser height. Be careful to consider the finish floor heights, which may differ top and bottom.

3. **FIND TREAD WIDTH**

   Check plans for tread width.

4. **CHECK HEADROOM**

   Chalk a line from edge of nosing at top of stairs to edge of nosing at bottom of stairs (see "Checking Stair Headroom" in the next pages of this chapter). Check for minimum clearance of 6'-8" to finish straight up from line to bottom of headroom.

5. **DRAW AND CUT STRINGERS**

   (See "Checking Stair Headroom.")

6. **CUT**

   Cut stringer spacers, treads, and risers.

7. **NAIL STRINGER SPACER**

   Nail stringer spacer to stringer. Spacer leaves clearance for applying wall finish.

8. **SET STRINGERS**

   a. At top deck measure down riser height plus tread thickness and mark for top of stringer.

   b. Set stringers to mark.

   c. Check stringers for level by placing a tread on top and bottom and checking level side to side and front to back.

   d. Adjust stringers for level.

   e. Nail stringers.

9. **NAIL RISERS**
10. **GLUE AND NAIL TREADS**

Finding Riser and Tread Dimensions when Not Given on Plans

If the riser and tread dimensions are not given on the plan, then you need to calculate them. To do this you should consider the following points:

- You want the steps to feel comfortable.

- When walking up steps, a person's mind determines the height of the riser based on the first step. Make sure all risers and treads are equal, so the stairs will not cause people to fall.

- The lower the riser, the longer the tread needs to be to feel comfortable.

- Common dimensions for riser and tread are 7" rise and 10½" tread.

- Use the following three rules to check to see if your stair dimensions are in the comfortable range.

    — Rule 1: Two risers and one tread added should equal 24" to 25".

    — Rule 2: One riser and one tread added should equal 17" to 18".

    — Rule 3: Multiply one riser by one tread and the result should equal 71" to 75".

Important Stair Code Regulations
2000 International Residential Code (IRC)
2000 International Building Code (IBC)

Width – 36" minimum – with occupant load of 49 or less (measured in clear, to finish).

44" minimum – with occupant load of 50 or more (measured in clear, to finish).

Rise – 4" minimum.

7¾" maximum for IRC – 7" for IBC, with residential 7¾".

Tread – 10" minimum for IRC – 11" for IBC with residential 10".

Riser height and tread length variance – ³/₈" maximum between the greatest and smallest within any flight of stairs.

Headroom – 6'-8" minimum, measured vertically from a line created by connecting the nosing of the stair treads to the soffit above.

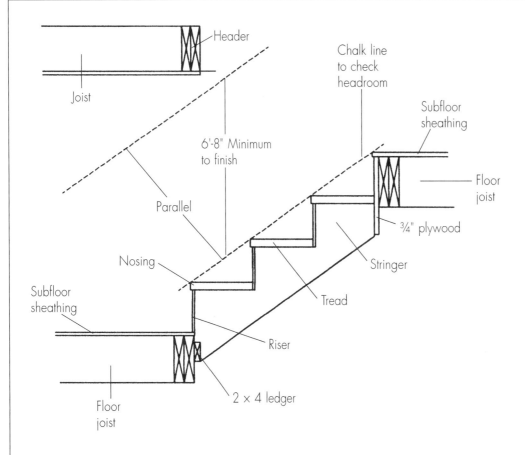

Header

Joist

Chalk line
to check
headroom

Subfloor
sheathing

6'-8" Minimum
to finish

Floor
joist

Parallel

¾" plywood

Nosing

Stringer

Tread

Subfloor
sheathing

Riser

Floor
joist

2 × 4 ledger

Checking Headroom before Stairs Are Built

First measure up from the subfloor sheathing at the bottom of the stair the height of one riser; then measure back the distance of the nosing and make a mark. From that mark, measure out parallel to the subfloor a distance equal to the combined width of the total number of treads and measure perpendicular to the subfloor the height of the total number of risers and make a second mark. Chalk a line between these two marks. From this line you can measure up to see if there are any obstructions in the headroom.

Measure treads and risers using framing square.

Subtract thickness of riser from top.

Notch bottom for ledger or stop plate. Notches differ (see above and the following page).

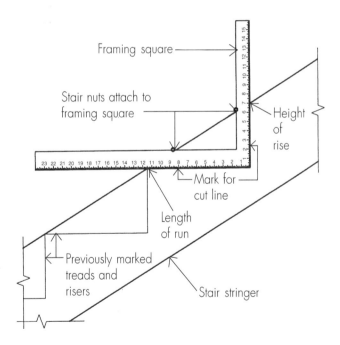

Care must be taken when marking the top and bottom steps. The thickness of the stair tread and the type of finish flooring on both the tread and the floor must be considered so that all the risers will be the same.

For the top tread be sure to figure in the riser so that the treads and nosings are all equal.

Standard Stair (To be Carpeted)

Adapt for use when plans do not give details.

2 × 12 Stair tread
- Router nosing with ½" round router bit.
- Glue and nail three 16d nails each stringer for single residence use.
- Glue and nail four 16d nails each stringer for multi-residence use.

Subfloor sheathing

Floor joist

1 × Riser
two 8d nails
each stringer

¾" plywood

Nail through plywood
to stringer and
stringer spacer.

Nosing

2 × 12 Stair stringer
- Two stringers for single residence use, 36" or less width.
- Three stringers for multi-residence use, or treads larger than 36".

Nail stringer to wall at each stud.

Stringer spacer — attach to side of stringer (2 × 4 normally used).

If stringers are not attached to walls, notch stringers for bottom stop plate.

Chapter Seven

Layout

Layout is the written language of the framer. If the lead framer "writes" clearly, then the framer reading the layout will be able to understand and properly perform the work. The layout person should include enough information in the layout so that the framer does not have to ask any questions. Layout language has been developed by framers over the years, and there are some variations. The version described in this manual is quite typical. Feel free to make any changes which reflect practices in your area. If you need to explain something about the layout that isn't shown in this chapter, either write it out on the plates in plain English, or explain it to the person who will do the framing.

Chapter ten provides a page with formulas for finding stud heights for different height foundations. This page may at first look a little complicated. However, after a closer look, you will find that by using the "Jobsite Worksheet" you can turn the difficult and often confusing job of finding stud heights into a fairly simple task.

Contents

Wall Layout Language

	Layout	**Studs** (Cutaway, looking down on wall from above)
Corner	`COR`	
Backer		
Stud trimmer	`X` `T`	
Double corner	`D COR`	
Double backer	`DB`	
Stud	`X`	
Double stud	`X` `X`	
Staggered studs	`U` `D` `U` `D` U = Up D = Down	
Beam	`81⅛T` `X` `T` `T` Write trimmer height (T) next to layout	

Nonbearing flat header	36" F
Nonbearing L-header	39" L
Nonbearing cripple header, more than 4'	60" C
Bearing walls, solid header, sizes vary	39" (4 × 8)

Header layout	`X` `T` `34"-(4 × 8) 35"C` `C` `T` `X`
	`X` `T` `C` `C` `C` `C` `T` `X`
	C = Cripple

Wall Layout

Wall layout is the process of taking the information given on the plans and writing enough instructions, in layout language, on the top and bottom plates so the framer can build the wall without asking any questions.

There is some general information that must be considered before starting. These items are listed below. Unless otherwise noted, all layout discussions will assume 2 × 4 studs at 16" O.C. (on center).

Where possible, we want joists, studs, and rafters to set directly over each other.

Before layout is started, establish reference points in the building for measuring both directions of layout and use those points for joist, stud, and rafter/truss layout throughout the building. Check the building plans for special joist plan or rafter/truss plans indicating layout. Select a reference point which allows you to lay out in as long and straight a line as possible, and which ensures that a maximum number of rafters/trusses are directly supported by studs.

Wall Layout Steps

1. Spread top plate and bottom plate together in chalk lines. If plate is not long enough, cut top plate to break on middle of stud and four feet away from walls running into it.
2. Place plates in position with chalk lines.
3. Lay out for backers from chalk lines.
4. Lay out stud trimmers and cripples for windows and doors.
5. Lay out studs.

Chalking Lines

"Chalking lines" is the process of marking on the subfloor where the walls are to be placed. Red chalk makes a permanent line and is easily seen. Blue chalk can be erased and is good to use if the lines might have to be changed. Using different colors allows you to distinguish between old and new lines.

Before chalking, when possible, check foundation and floor for square. Walls must be square, plumb, and level. If necessary, adjust your chalk lines accordingly.

Measurements for chalk lines are derived from wall dimensions as given in the plans. If the plans show finished walls, be sure to subtract the appropriate amount to get your framing measurements.

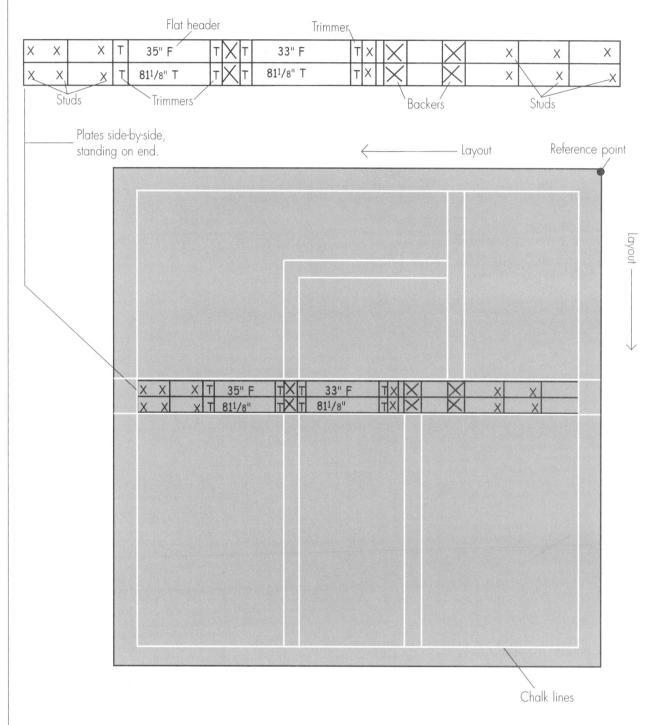

Chalk lines on subfloor sheathing using dimensions on plans.

Pulling Layout from a Corner (16" O.C.)

Pull layout so that sheathing will break in the middle of a joist/stud. Hook tape on the outside edge of rim joist/plate. Pull and locate 16" on tape, then measure back half the thickness of joist/stud (¾" for 2× stock) and mark. This puts the layout mark on 15¼". Make an "X" on the correct side of the layout mark to show the location of the joist/stud. Continue marking in this way for each subsequent 16" space, thus: 31¼", 47¼", 63¼", etc. Finish by drawing square lines through the mark.

The reason for subtracting the ¾" is that the 4' × 8' sheathing will be installed from the *outside edge* of the rim joist/plate, not from the center.

Pulling from an Existing Layout (16" O.C.)

Set end of tape on a layout mark, pull and mark 16", 32", 48", etc. Make an "X" on the correct side of the layout mark and square a line through the mark. For a long span, set a nail on the existing layout mark, hook tape on the nail, and pull layout.

Joist Layout

Joist layout is the process of taking the information given on the plans and writing enough instructions on the top of the rim joist or double plate so the joist framer can spread and nail the joists without asking any questions.

Where possible, we want joists, studs, and rafters to set directly over each other.

Before layout is started, establish reference points in the building for measuring both directions of layout and use those points for joist, stud, and rafter/truss layout throughout the building. Check the building plans for special joist plan or rafter/truss plans indicating layout. Select a reference point which allows you to lay out in as long and straight a line as possible, and which ensures that a maximum number of rafters/trusses are directly supported by studs.

Check plans for openings in the floor required for stairs, chimneys, etc.

Check plans for bearing partitions on the floor. Double joists under bearing partitions running parallel.

Check locations of toilets to see if joists must be headed out for toilet drain pipe.

Joist Layout Language

Joist	X
Tail joist	T
Double joist	X X
Beam	6 x 12

Joist Layout Steps

1. Layout for double joist, trimmer joist, and tail joist.
2. Layout for other joists.

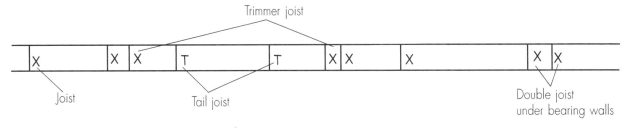

98

Roof Layout

Roof layout is the process of taking the information given on the plans and writing enough instructions on the double plate for the roof framer to spread and nail the rafters or trusses.

Use the same reference points established for floor and wall building for starting layout on the roof.

Roof rafters and trusses are sometimes 24" O.C. as compared with 16" O.C. for floors and walls. In that case, only every third truss or rafter will be over a stud.

Before layout is started, check plans for openings in the roof required by dormers, skylights, chimneys, etc.

For roof trusses, lay out according to truss plan, especially for hip-truss packages.

Roof Layout Language

Rafter or truss	X
Tail rafter or truss	T
Double rafter or truss	X X

Roof Layout Steps

1. Layout for doubles, trimmers, and tail rafters or trusses.
2. Layout for other rafters or trusses.

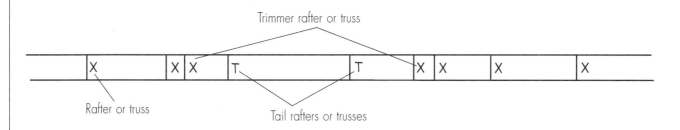

Chapter Eight

Managing a Framing Team

Management techniques have been developed over the years by studying and applying methods that work. The trend has been away from the dominating "command" approach and toward the cooperative "team" approach. This chapter deals with some organizational tasks, as well as with relationships and motivation. Developing good working relationships and instilling motivation is probably the most important and the most difficult task of a leader. A construction project manned by crews of skilled craftsmen who take pride in their work and get along with each other is bound to be successful. Assembling and directing such crews can only be accomplished by a leader who has developed good management skills.

Contents

Lead Framers

A Lead Framer Must Possess:
1. Knowledge to frame any building.
2. Ability to impart knowledge to other framers.
3. Ability to motivate other framers.

1. Knowledge to Frame Any Building

As a lead framer, you must thoroughly understand the basic concepts involved in framing any style building. The framing crew takes their direction from you; you, in turn, take your direction, depending on the situation, from any of the following:

a. Framing contractor
b. Site superintendent
c. Architect or engineer
d. Owner

There are a number of framing requirements that are easy to overlook. Compile a checklist of such items and refer to it during each phase of the job. For example:

Framing checklist

WALLS:	• Studs for tubs, medicine cabinets, etc.
	• Special shear nailing
	• Hold-downs
	• Alignment of windows and doors
	• Size of studs
JOISTS:	• Heading-off for toilets
	• Double under bearing walls
	• Cantilevering overhangs
ROOF:	• Fascia overhang 6" for gutters
	• Skylights or roof hatch
	• Ventilation
	• Attic access
CRAWL SPACE:	• Vents in rim joists
	• Crawl-space access

2. Ability to Impart Knowledge to Other Framers

• When teaching someone, start with the basics. Assume nothing. Explain in clear and simple language exactly what the job is and how it is to be done.

• The easiest way to lead is to give orders, make demands, and threaten punishment. However, it creates an unsettling atmosphere which is not conducive to a cooperative, self-motivated crew. *Request* that framers do tasks; do not *order* them.

- Assume that no framer intentionally does something wrong. Do not be dogmatic or negative when you point out mistakes. Help him correct the error and show him how to avoid making it again.

- Treat each framer with respect. His time may be less valuable to the company, but his worth as an individual is equal to yours.

- The words, "please" and "thank-you," can make a framer feel much better about working for you. It is an easy way to let him know that what he does is important and appreciated.

- Do not give the hard, unpleasant jobs to the same framer time after time. The entire crew should share such tasks.

- When a framer asks you a question, give him the answer, but then explain how you got the answer so the next time he can figure it out himself.

3. Ability to Motivate Other Framers

To produce good work efficiently, a framer must be motivated.

To be motivated, a framer must:
A) Feel good about himself.
B) Feel what he is doing is important.
C) Be respected by his lead framer.
D) Feel he is being treated equally.

A) *Feel good about himself.*

You are a lead framer, not a therapist, but your attitude toward your crew, as exemplified in items B, C, and D, should have a positive effect in this regard. A crew whose members take pride in their individual and collective skills will invariably produce quality work and take pleasure in doing it.

B) *Feel what he is doing is important.*

Every task, no matter how small, is necessary to complete the job and, therefore, important.

C) *Be respected by his lead framer.*

1. Take time to listen and teach. If as lead framer, you are called upon to solve a framing problem, it is better to let the framer explain his solution first and, if it is an acceptable solution, let him do it his way. There are often several ways to solve a framing problem. If you have a way that is much faster or easier than the framer's way, explain it to him and tell him how you came to your conclusion.

2. Directions should be given in terms of the job, not the individual. For example: *Negative*—"I told you five minutes ago to build that wall." *Positive*—"We need that wall built right away so we can finish this unit."

3. Framers like to feel the person supervising is concerned about what they think and how they feel. Convey this through your words and actions.

D) *Feel he is being treated equally.*

Don't show favoritism when assigning tasks. Make every effort to treat all framers fairly and take time to impartially deal with any complaints that might arise.

Goals for Motivation

Goals are excellent motivational tools. When assigning each task, specify a goal for its completion within a certain amount of time.

Goals help you to:
1. Determine how fast you are getting work done.
2. Think of faster ways of getting work done.
3. Maintain the motivation to work faster.
4. Pass the day.

Goals should, of course, be realistic and attainable.

Develop three sets of goals:
1. Task goals (frame this wall in two hours).
2. Daily goals (frame and set six walls today).
3. Project goals (frame this building in three weeks).

Each framer should set his own daily goals. The lead framer should review them and, if the time assigned seems too long, should suggest ways to make the task easier or faster. A framer's value to the company, and thus his wages, are commensurate with his ability to produce work that is high in both quantity and quality; if you produce more, you earn more. Making this fact clear to each member of your crew is, perhaps, the best motivation of all.

Company Goals
1. To provide income for framers and the company.
2. To provide a safe and enjoyable work environment.
3. To produce high-quality framed buildings.
4. To develop framing skills and abilities.
5. To build up the company.
6. To create comradeship among the framers.
7. To coordinate with the general contractor's schedule and needs.

Lead Framers *(continued)*

It is great to have a team of framers working together and doing such a good and fast job that they feel good about themselves and the company they are a part of. This creates the desire to improve themselves and the company because they not only get positive feedback, but earn more money.

Framing Contractor Tasks

The framing contractor is, in many cases, also the lead framer. The following tasks are his responsibility.

1. Check location and quality of power supply.
2. Check location and date of lumber drop.
3. Check window delivery schedule.
4. Check truss delivery schedule when appropriate.
5. Arrange to have the builder complete as much site preparation as possible before starting, including leveling the area around the building where framers will be working.
6. Highlight items on plans that are easy to miss or hard to find.
7. Give the lead framer a list of potential problem areas and items that are easy to forget.

Chapter Nine

Costs, Equipment, and Material Handling

The aim of this chapter is to show how a number of organized management procedures can be integrated into the daily job routine. All these procedures have as their goal maximum productivity at minimal cost. Every member of a framing crew should be constantly aware of this goal and actively work to achieve it. For example, it is important that a framer be conscious of the value and cost of his time and of the materials he works with. When a framer drops a handful of nails, knowing the cost of those nails will help him decide whether it's worthwhile to break his flow and bend down and pick up the nails, or keep on working and forget about them. If a framer knows the actual time saved by a quick, as opposed to a relaxed walk, perhaps he will be convinced to pick up the pace.

The organization and handling of material is an often overlooked, and yet very important, aspect of framing productivity. It is amazing how much time and money can be saved by a little planning and applied common sense.

Contents

Objective: To frame a quality building for the least possible cost. Wages represent the greatest percentage of the total cost, and since wages are paid for time spent working, it follows that if you lessen the time it takes to complete a building, you thereby reduce the wages paid and, thus, lower the total cost.

There are various tasks involved in framing. Some of the tasks can be done as fast or nearly as fast by the least experienced framer as by the most experienced framer, for example, carrying and spreading studs. Suppose that a $10/hour person can do the same job as a $20/hour person, only 20% slower. You save $8/hour by having the less expensive person do the job.

Be careful, however, because if an inexperienced framer takes on a job beyond his capabilities, the chances for mistakes are great. This could result in wages paid for work incorrectly done, and higher wages paid for an experienced framer to find and correct the mistake.

It is ideal for you to have a balanced crew of experienced and inexperienced framers. This allows you the flexibility to fit the framer to the task. It takes planning to coordinate framing tasks so that they are done as inexpensively as possible, but it is time well spent for the money you will save.

The following are job titles and responsibilities for a typical large framing crew, divided into four categories.

Organizing

1) **Lead framer**	– Coordinate work schedule with framing contractor.
	– Locate lumber drop.
	– Make sure tools and supplies are available.
	– Train framers.
	– Solve problems.
2) **Cut and chalk framer**	– Cut stairs and rafters.
	– Chalk lines.
	– Assign framers to tasks.
3) **Layout framer**	– Layout for walls, joists, rafters, and trusses.

Walls

1) **Plumb and line framer**	– Plumb and line walls.
2) **Wall spreader**	– Spread all parts of a wall (studs, trimmers, cripples, headers, etc.) so they are ready to be nailed together.

3) **Wall nailer**   – Nail walls together.

4) **Makeup framer**   – Nail together a quantity of stud-trimmers, corners, backers, headers, etc., before they are carried to the walls.

Floors

Joisting

1) **Rim joister**   – Nail joists in position.
     – Header out joists.

2) **Joist nailer**   – Nail joists in position.
     – Nail on joist hangers.
     – Nail blocking and drywall backing.

3) **Joist spreader**   – Carry joists into place.

Sheathing

1) **Sheathing setter**   – Place and set sheathing.

2) **Sheathing nailer**   – Glue joists ahead of setter and nail sheathing behind setter.

3) **Sheathing carrier**   – Carry sheathing to setter.

Roofs

1) **Spreaders**   – Spread and install trusses and rafters.
     – Install fascia.

2) **Blockers**   – Install blocking and drywall backing.
     – Set sheathing.

3) **Sheathing packers**   – Carry sheathing to setters.

Multiple Framer Tasks

Some tasks require more than one framer, for example, lifting large walls. Any time framers have to be called from other tasks to perform a common task, much care must be taken not to waste time. The cost per minute of a 5-framer task is 5 times that of a single framer task. The person organizing the task needs to take responsibility for making sure the task is ready for all framers. If it is lifting a wall, the organizing framer should make sure the wall is completely ready so framers don't stand around while one makes last minute adjustments.

Learning Curve

Studies have been done which show that as output is doubled, the time required decreases according to a constant ratio. The common ratio is about 4 to 5, or 20%. For example, the fourth set of stairs built will take 20% less time than the second.

Multiple Cutting Analysis

Multiple cutting becomes efficient when you have to cut a number of pieces of lumber the same size. Trimmers, cripples, and blocks are good examples.

To multiple cut, first spread all the lumber to be cut out on the floor or a table. Then measure each piece, mark each piece with your square, and finally cut each piece.

Analysis has shown it takes 36% less time to cut ten pieces of 2 × 4 when the tasks of spreading, then measuring, then marking, and then cutting are done for all the pieces at one time.

For very large numbers of cuts it may be worthwhile to make a template or a measuring/cutting jig.

Motion Analysis

Question: Can significant time (and money) be saved by moving faster?

Motion analysis studies of framers produced the following results for different speeds over a given distance.

Relaxed walk .... 148 seconds
Quick walk .... 117 seconds
Nail pouch shuffle .... 84 seconds
Drop the nail pouch and run .... 63 seconds

Example: Let's suppose a framer walks 2 hours in an 8-hour day. If a framer does a quick walk instead of a relaxed walk, 25 minutes would be saved during the day. The nail pouch shuffle would save 52 minutes.

Conclusion: A quick pace pays.

Speed Versus Quality

Speed or quality: Which should it be? How good must the work be if it must be done as fast as possible? The two variables to consider when answering these questions are:

- Strength
- Attractiveness

First and most important is the structural integrity of the building. The second is creating a finished frame that will be pleasing to the eye. Once requirements for strength and attractiveness are satisfied, the faster the job can be done, the better.

Material Movement

Framing requires a lot of material movement. It is estimated that one-quarter to one-third of a framer's time is spent moving material, so any time or energy saved is a cost reduction.

The following hints will help you save time, energy, motion, and in the last analysis, money.

- Whenever material is lifted or moved, it takes time and energy; therefore, move material as little as possible.
- When stacking lumber, consider the following:
  —Where will it be used next?
  —Will it be close to where it is going to be used?
  —Will it be in the way of another operation?
  —Will it obstruct a pathway?
- Always stack material neatly. This helps to keep the lumber straight and makes it easy for framers to pick up and carry it. Stack 2 x 4 studs in piles of eight for a convenient armful.
- Have second-floor lumber dumped close to the building so framers can stand on the lumber stack and throw it onto the second floor.
- When stacking lumber on a deck, place it where walls will not be built so it will not have to be moved again.
- Use mechanical aids, such as levers, for lifting. Remember your physics — the longer the handle in relation to the lifting arm, the easier it will be to lift the load.
- Two trips to the lumber stack or tool truck cost twice as much as one trip. If you have to go to the tool truck for a tool, check to see if you need nails or anything else.

Tool Maintenance Schedule

Draw up a schedule such as this for your specific equipment; post it, and assign a reliable crew member to take charge of it.

Equipment	Schedule	Maintenance Operation	Lubrication
Worm-drive saw	First of every month	Check oil	Heavy-duty saw lubricant
Nail guns	Each day before using	Oil	Gun oil
Compressors	Before using every day	Check oil	30-weight non-detergent
	Every Friday	Empty air and drain tanks	
	First of each month	Check air-intake filter	
	Every month	Change oil	30-weight non-detergent
Electric cords	First of each month	Test cords color code	

Nail Costs (approximate)

Nail	Cost per Box	Cost per Nail
16d	$15	½ cent
8d	$16	¼ cent
16d box galvanized	$25	1¼ cent
1½" roofing	$25	⅓ cent
2½" concrete	$1.20/lb	1⅔ cents
10d x .131 gun	$28	½ cent
8d gun	$28	½ cent
1½" roofing gun	$42	⅔ cent
1¾" gun staple	$50	½ cent
Shot and pin	—	38 cents

Chapter Ten

Codes, Standards and Safety

Building code books are the ruling authorities when it comes to questions of framing. However, codes are vast in scope and contain thousands of items which are of no use to the average framer. The code guides in this chapter make it easy for framers to locate in the two code books, the important things they need to know.

Starting with the year 2000, the three code associations in the U.S. combined to create one code. This code is presented as the International Residential Code and International Building Code. The International Residential Code covers one- and two-family dwellings and the International Building Code covers all buildings.

The "Standard Framing Dimensions" tables were developed to ensure the consistency and compatibility of all dimensions within a specific framing project. These tables can, of course, be adapted to any given stud height. When making your own table, be sure to double-check your calculations and review the dimensions with the builder. Mistakes are easier and less costly to eliminate before the job begins than to correct after framing members have been cut and nailed in place.

"Framing Terms" have all been defined by a framer for framers, and are as straightforward as possible.

Contents

Subject	Section	Table/Figure	Page
Attic access	R807		249
Beams and girders bearing	R606.13		173
Beam notches	R502.8.1		84
Chimneys and Fireplaces			
Clearance	R1001.15 & R1003.12		263 & 268
Crickets	R1001.17		265
Fire blocking	R1001.16		264
Crawl-space clearance and access	R323.1 & R408.3		52 & 78
Crawl-space ventilation	R408.1 & R408.2		78
Decay protection	R323	R301.2 (7)	36 & 52-53
Engineered wood products (I-joists)	R502.1.4 & R502.8.2		79 & 84
Fire blocking	R602.8		112
Draft stopping	R502.12		86
Floors			
Joists around openings	R502.10	R502.2	80 & 86
Joists bearing	R502.6		79
Joists bridging and blocking	R502.7	R502.2	80 & 84
Joists drilling and notching	R502.8	R502.8	84-85
Joist hangers	R502.6.2		79
Joists lapping	R502.6.1	R502.2	79-80
Joists under bearing walls	R502.4		79
Minimum emergency opening sizes	R310		47
Nailing		R602.3 (1)	104-105
Roof and Ceilings			
Bearing	R802.6		217
Ceiling height	R305		43
Ceiling joists lap	R802.3.2		213
Connection-rafter and ceiling joist	R802.3.1	R802.5.1 (9)	213 & 234
Cutting, notching and drilling	R802.7		217

Subject	Section	Table/Figure	Page
Attic access	1208.2		262
Beams and girders bearing	2304.11.2.4		551
Chimneys and Fireplaces			
Fireplace clearance	2111.12		527
Chimney clearance	2113.11.2.6 & 2113.19		530 & 532
Fire blocking	2111.14 & 2113.20		527 & 532
Crawl-space clearance and access	1208.1 & 2304.11.2.1		262 & 551
Crawl-space ventilation	1202.3		259
Decay protection	2304.11		551-552
Engineered wood products (I-joists)	2303.1.2		541
Fire blocking	716.2		115
Draft stopping	716.3 & .4		116-117
Floors			
Joists around openings	2308.8.3		572
Joists bearing	2308.8.1		572
Joists bridging and blocking	2308.8.2 & 2308.8.5		572
Joists drilling and notching	2308.8.2		572
Joist hangers	2308.8.2		572
Joists under bearing walls	2308.8.4		572
Minimum emergency opening sizes	1009		246-247
Nailing	2304.9	2304.9.1	547-550
Roof and Ceilings			
Ceiling height	1207.2		261
Ceiling joists lap	2308.10.4.1		589
Connection-rafter and ceiling joist	2308.10.4.1		589
Cutting, notching and drilling	2308.10.4.2		589
Rafters around openings	2308.10.4.3		589
Rafters bridging and blocking	2308.8.5 & 2308.10.6		572 & 589
Wood trusses	2308.10.7		589
Ventilation	1202.2		259

Subject	Section	Table/Figure	Page
Ridge board	2308.10.4		589
Spans			
Ceiling joists	2308.10.2	2308.10.2 (1) & (2)	580-582
Floor joists	2308.8	2308.8 (1) & (2)	569-571
Girders and headers	2308.9.5.1	2308.9.5 & 2308.9.6	577-579
Sheathing		2304.6.1 & 2304.7 (1) - (5)	544-546
Rafters	2308.10.3	2308.10.3 (1) - (6)	580 & 583-588
Stairways	1003.3.3		225-228
Guards	1003.2.12		217
Handrails	1003.3.3.11		227-228
Stair landings	1003.3.3.4		226
Ramps	1003.3.4		228-229
Exits	1004-1006		230-240
Termite protection	2304.11.6		552
Walls			
Anchorage	2308.3.3 & 2308.6		569
Bracing	2308.3 & 2308.9.3	2308.9.3 (1)	569, 573-574, 577
Cripple walls	2308.9.4		577
Double plate	2308.9.2.1		573
Drilling or notching studs	2308.9.10 & 11		580
Non-bearing headers	2308.9.7		579
Stud spacing	2308.9.1	2308.9.1	572-573
Additional seismic Category B or C	2308.11		591
Additional seismic Category D or E	2308.12		591

Finding Stud Heights for Different Height Foundations

SH = Stud Height
TRD = Transit Reading Down
TRU = Transit Reading Up
SB = Stud Base

Equations

SH = TRD + SB

SH = SB − TRU

Steps

1. Set the bottom plate.
2. Find SB (stud base) by looking on the plans for height of wall; then subtract the height of the "Transit reading from floor" and the 3" for top and double plate.

Job Site Worksheet

	TRD	+	SB	=	SH
SH1		+		=	
SH2		+		=	
SH3		+		=	
SH4		+		=	
SH5		+		=	
SH6		+		=	
	SB	−	TRU	=	
SH7		−		=	
SH8		−		=	
SH9		−		=	
SI I10		−		=	
SH11		−		=	
SH12		−		=	

Standard Framing Dimensions 88⅝" Studs

		Header Size	Trimmer Size* ** ***
Stud height .... 88⅝"			
Wall height .... 93⅛"			
R.O. windows................. Width—nominal			
Height—nominal		4 x 8	81⅛"
		4 x 10	79⅛"
R.O. exterior doors .... Width—nominal + 2½"			
Height—82⅝"		4 x 8	81⅛"
Height—82⅛"		4 x 10	80⅝" cut T.P.
R.O. sliding glass doors .... Width—nominal			
Height—6'-10" door 82⅛"		4 x 8	81⅛"/ ½" furr
82⅛"		4 x 10	80⅝" cut T.P.
Height—6'-8" door 80⅛"		4 x 8	81⅛"/ 2½" furr
80⅛"		4 x 10	79⅛ / ½" furr
R.O. interior doors .... Width—nominal + 2"			
(nonbearing) Height—82⅝"			81⅛"
R.O. bifold doors .... Width —nominal + 1¼" for ½" drywall —nominal + 1½" for ⅝" drywall			
Height — 82⅝ "			81⅛"
R.O. bypass doors .... Width—nominal			
Height—82⅝"			81⅛"
R.O. pocket doors .... Width — 2 x nominal + 1"			
Height—84½"			83"
Bathtubs...................... Width—nominal + ¼"			
Tub fire blocks .... 14½" from finish floor to bottom of block			
Medicine-cabinet blocks .... R.O. 14½" x 24"			
Height—48" from finish floor to bottom of R.O. 3" minimum away from wall corner			

These dimensions should be checked with the job-site superintendent before beginning each job.

* Furr = furring under header after header is in place.

** Trimmer heights will increase by 1½" if lightweight concrete is used or ¾" if gypcrete is used.

*** Cut T.P. —Cut the top plate out and leave the double plate.

R.O. (rough opening) – Any opening framed by the framing members.

Standard Framing Dimensions 92⁵/₈" Studs

		Header Size	Trimmer Size* **
Stud height .... 92⁵/₈"			
Wall height .... 97¹/₈"			
R.O. windows .... Width—nominal			
Height—nominal		4 x 8	85¹/₈"
		4 x 10	83¹/₈"
R.O. exterior doors .... Width—nominal + 2½"			
Height—82⁵/₈"		4 x 8	85¹/₈"/4" furr
Height—82⁵/₈"		4 x 10	83¹/₈"/2" furr cut T.P.
R.O. sliding glass doors .... Width—nominal			
Height—6'10" door	82¹/₈"	4 x 8	85¹/₈"/4½" furr
	82¹/₈"	4 x 10	83¹/₈"/2½" furr
Height—6'8" door	80¹/₈"	4 x 8	85¹/₈"/6½" furr
	80¹/₈"	4 x 10	83¹/₈"/4½" furr
R.O. interior doors .... Width—nominal + 2"			
(nonbearing) Height—82⁵/₈"			81¹/₈"
R.O. bifold doors	Width — nominal + 1¼" for ½" drywall — nominal + 1½" for ⁵/₈" drywall		
Height — 82⁵/₈"			81¹/₈"
R.O. bypass doors .... Width—nominal			
Height—82⁵/₈"			81¹/₈"
R.O. pocket doors .... Width — 2 x nominal + 1"			
Height—84½"			83"
Bathtubs .... Width—nominal + ¼"			
Tub fire blocks .... 14½" from finish floor to bottom of block			
Medicine-cabinet .... R.O. 14½" x 24"			
blocks Height—48" from finish floor to bottom of R.O. 3" minimum away from wall corner			

These dimensions should be checked with the job-site superintendent before beginning each job.

* Furr = furring under header after header is in place.

** Trimmer heights will increase by 1½" if lightweight concrete is used or ¾" if gypcrete is used.

R.O. (rough opening) —Any opening framed by the framing members.

To adapt the standard framing dimensions to other stud heights, the following apply:

- All widths will be the same.

- The height for the windows will be nominal. To determine the trimmer size, just find the height of the bottom of the header and subtract 1½" for the bottom plate.

- To determine the height of the window and, thereby, the amount of furring, you need to look on the plans. Usually the height can be found on the elevations. However, it can also appear on the floor plans. If the height is not given, use the door height for the window height.

- For exterior doors, furr down to 82⅝" from the subfloor sheathing.

- For sliding glass doors: – 6'-10" furr down to 82"
  – 6'-8" furr down to 80".

- All else remains the same.

Header Length for Doors

Common Wood Doors

Door size	+ Jam shim allowance	+ Trimmer width	= Header size
Examples			
Interior 2⁶ door (30")	+ 2"	+ 3"	= 35"
Exterior 3⁰ door (36")	+ 2½"	+ 3"	= 41½"

Header Length for Windows

Aluminum or Vinyl Nail-Flange Windows

Window size	+Trimmer width	= Header size
Examples		
3° (36")	+ 3"	= 39"
8° (96")	+ 6"	= 102"

Trimmer Height

Use the standard $81\frac{1}{8}$" trimmer height for a standard $82\frac{5}{8}$" opening.
The trimmer height must be adjusted for the following.

1. Special door sizes.
2. Special floor coverings that go on top of the subfloor and are applied before the doors are hung, such as lightweight concrete or gypcrete.

Bathroom Framing Dimensions

Where bathtub plumbing occurs, place studs at 8", 24", and approximately 32" from back wall (depending on width of tub) to allow space for piping.

Check medicine cabinets for spacing studs. Common medicine cabinet spacing is 14½" between studs and at least 3" from a corner. A standard opening is usually 24" from top to bottom and begins 48" from the floor.

Toilet Clearance

These are common dimensions, but should be checked with the builder.

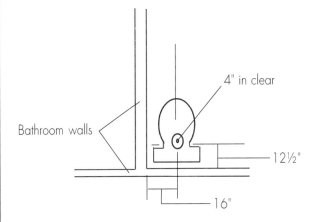

Safety Tips

1. Keep work area neat underfoot, especially main pathways.

2. Keep work areas well lighted and adequately ventilated.

3. Don't leave nails sticking out; pull them or bend them over.

4. When lifting, always lift using your leg muscles and not your back. Always keep your back straight, your chin tucked in, and your stomach pulled in. Don't carry objects resting against your stomach; this will cause your spine to bend backward. Maintain the same posture when setting objects down. (See illustration.)

5. When working on joists, trusses, or rafters, always watch each step to see that what you are stepping on is secure.

6. Never pin circular saw guards back.

7. Do not wear loose or torn clothing that can get caught in tools.

8. Wear heavy shoes or boots that help protect your feet against injury.

9. Wear hard hats where material or tools can fall on your head.

10. Wear safety glasses where there is any potential for injury to the eye.

11. Use hearing protection when operating loud machinery or when hammering in a small, enclosed space.

12. Wear a dust mask for protection from sawdust, insulation fibers, or the like.

13. Use a respirator whenever working in exposure to toxic fumes.

14. Assign a qualified person to regularly inspect the job site.

15. Make first aid supplies available and make sure they are replenished on a regular basis.

16. Post location and number of the closest medical facility.

Fall Protection Tips

Most deaths in the construction industry happen as a result of falls. Falls also cause many of the injuries that occur on the job site, according to OSHA (the Occupational Safety and Health Administration).

Because framing can place you a story or more off the ground it's important to work safely and to become aware of fall protection equipment, as well as systems (such as guardrails, safety nets, and covers) that can help prevent falls.

Below are some safety tips on equipment and systems. Using these can help protect yourself and others on the job site from falls.

The Full-body Harness

When you're working on a roof or a leading edge of a deck, where you are exposed to a fall, a full body harness should be worn. The harness needs to be attached to a secure anchor. This can be done with a lanyard, rope-grab ascender, a lead rope or a retractable lifeline. An ascender or retractable lifeline grabs tightly when downward pressure is exerted (like the pressure of your weight if you fall).

Safety with Ladders

Improper use of ladders is the number one cause of falls. The base of ladders should be on flat surfaces and kept clear of debris.

Remember with **stepladders,** the higher you go, the more unstable the ladder becomes. Stepladders are not made to be leaned against walls. Make sure they are fully extended and locked into position.

A straight ladder should not be placed too steeply against the structure it is leaning on. Otherwise it may topple backward when someone is on it, especially near the top. When the ladder is used to get to a higher surface, the top of the ladder should extend three feet past the point of contact with the structure on which it is leaning, and the top should be secured to the structure.

Wooden ladders, although heavy, do not conduct electricity. They are the best choice if you are working around exposed electricity.

Site Safety

Covers and **guardrails** over and around any floor holes are often used on residential construction projects.

Guardrail top railings should be 39" to 45" from the working surface. The middle rails should be half the distance between the top rail and the working surface. Toe boards running along the edge of the working surface should be used wherever workers below are exposed to falling objects. The railings should be on the inside of the uprights and the uprights should not be more than 8' apart. The guardrails should be able to withstand 200 pounds of force in any direction.

In some instances, covers and guardrails may not be the best protection method. In these cases, it is important to understand the hazards associated with the specific job and to establish appropriate work site protective measures.

Some Rules to Follow:

When working on roof trusses/rafters, top plate scaffold brackets can be used to provide a walkway along the inside of the walls. These walkways can also be used for installing the first row of roof sheathing.

When applying roof materials, wear shoes that provide as much grip to surface as possible. Do not work in bad weather that would create a hazardous situation, and repair damaged portions of the roof deck as soon as possible.

When doing attic and roof work, do not work in bad weather. This often creates hazardous situations. Make sure that the material you use is located close to you. Finally, don't stand or walk beneath or next to any opening in the ceiling (something may fall out of the hole).

It is good to stop any construction operations above 6' during periods of bad weather: high winds, moisture, or icy surfaces create dangerous conditions and increase the risk of falls.

Appendix

SYMBOL	DEFINITION
— — — — — 123	EXISTING CONTOUR
———————— 124	NEW CONTOUR
—————— G ——————	GAS SERVICE LINE
—————— W ——————	WATER SERVICE LINE
—————— SS ——————	SANITARY SEWER LINE
—————— D ——————	DRAIN LINE
—————— E ——————	ELECTRIC SERVICE
—————— UE ——————	UNDERGROUND ELECTRIC SERVICE
—————— OE ——————	OVERHEAD ELECTRIC SERVICE
— — — — — — —	EXISTING WORK (GENERAL)
——— — ——— — ———	CONTRACT LIMIT LINE
✝ 12.34	SPOT GRADE
O— SMH #	SEWER MANHOLE #
O— DMH #	DRAIN MANHOLE #
☐— CB#	CATCH BASIN #
—▷◁—	VALVE
✦	BORING OR TEST PIT
BM 134.36	BENCH MARK ELEV.
✦	FIRE HYDRANT
O #	UTILITY POLE #
RIM = 34.56'	ELEV. OF MANHOLE RIM
INV. IN = 34.56'	ELEV. OF INVERT IN
INV. OUT = 34.56'	ELEV. OF INVERT OUT

SYMBOL	DEFINITION
	WALL SECTION NO.2 CAN BE SEEN ON DRAWING NO. A-4.
	DETAIL SECTION NO.3 CAN BE SEEN ON DRAWING NO. A-5.
	BUILDING SECTION A-A CAN BE SEEN ON DRAWING NO. A-6.
————————	MAIN OBJECT LINE
– – – – – – – –	HIDDEN OR INVISIBLE LINE
— — · — — · —	INDICATES CENTERLINE
→ 3" ← 3'-4"	DIMENSION LINES
↓ ↓	EXTENSION LINES
℄	SYMBOL INDICATES CENTER LINE
/////////////	INDICATES WALL SURFACE
◁——(N)——	INDICATES NORTH DIRECTION

SYMBOL	DEFINITION
(CL)———— — ——	COLUMN LINE GRID
⟨5⟩—— OR ▷5————	PARTITION TYPE
⬡ A	WINDOW TYPE
(05)	DOOR NUMBER
[05]	ROOM NUMBER
(10'-0")	CEILING HEIGHT
△2 ☁	REVISION MARKER
↦ ⊣ ⊢	BREAK IN A CONTINUOUS LINE
(3)——→	REFER TO NOTE #3
◐ 100'-0"	ELEVATION MARKER
◇ 1 / 4 A-5 2 / 3	INTERIOR ELEVATIONS 1, 2, 3, & 4 CAN BE SEEN ON DRWG. A-5. DIRECTION OF TRIANGLE INDICATES ELEVATION.

MATERIAL INDICATION SYMBOLS

MATERIAL	PLAN	ELEVATION	SECTION
EARTH	NONE	NONE	
POROUS FILL	NONE	NONE	
CONCRETE			SAME AS PLAN
BRICK			SAME AS PLAN
CONCRETE BLOCK			SAME AS PLAN
STONE	CUT STONE / RUBBLE	CUT STONE / RUBBLE	SAME AS PLAN
STEEL	OR / OR	NONE	
FRAMING WOOD	WALL OR PARTITION	SIDING / FINISH WOOD	BLOCKING / FRAMING
PLYWOOD	INDICATED BY NOTE	INDICATED BY NOTE	
SHEET METAL FLASHING	INDICATED BY NOTE		SHAPED HEAVY LINE

MATERIAL INDICATION SYMBOLS			
MATERIAL	PLAN	ELEVATION	SECTION
BATT INSULATION		NONE	SAME AS PLAN
RIGID INSULATION		NONE	SAME AS PLAN
GLASS			SMALL SCALE / LARGE SCALE
GYPSUM WALLBOARD			SAME AS PLAN
ACOUSTICAL TILE		NONE	
CERAMIC WALL TILE			SAME AS PLAN
FLOOR TILE		NONE	

WINDOW AND DOOR SYMBOLS

TYPE	PLAN	ELEVATION
DOUBLE HUNG WINDOWS		
CASEMENT WINDOW		INDICATES WINDOW HINGE
SLIDER		
EXTERIOR DOOR		
INTERIOR DOOR		
BIFOLD DOOR		

Plumbing Fixture Symbols

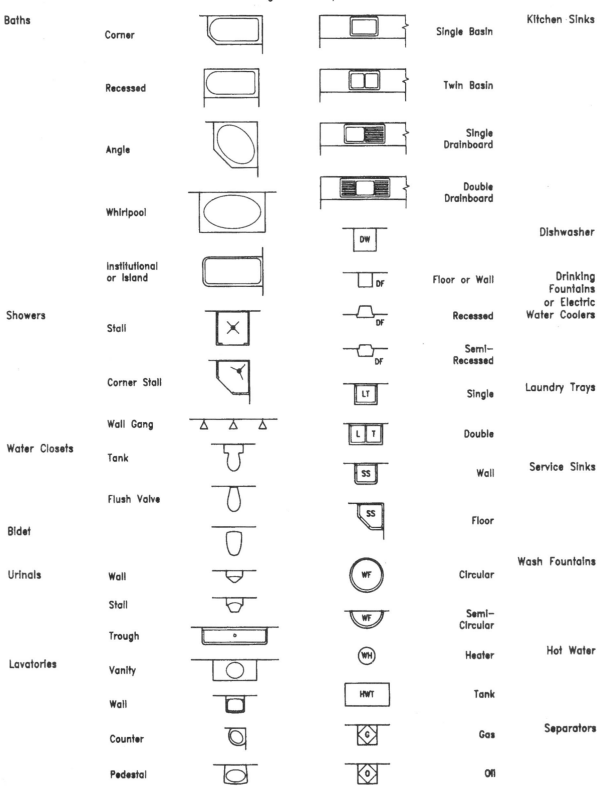

Baths		Kitchen Sinks
Corner		Single Basin
Recessed		Twin Basin
Angle		Single Drainboard
Whirlpool		Double Drainboard
Institutional or Island		Dishwasher
Showers		Drinking Fountains or Electric Water Coolers
Stall		Floor or Wall
		Recessed
		Semi-Recessed
Corner Stall		Single — Laundry Trays
Wall Gang		Double
Water Closets		Wall — Service Sinks
Tank		Floor
Flush Valve		
Bidet		Wash Fountains
Urinals		Circular
Wall		Semi-Circular
Stall		Heater — Hot Water
Trough		Tank
Lavatories		
Vanity		Gas — Separators
Wall		Oil
Counter		
Pedestal		

Glossary

Anchor bolt

A device for connecting wood members to concrete or masonry.

Backer

Three studs nailed together in a U-shape to which a partition is attached.

Bargeboard

Board attached to a gable rafter to which a rake board is attached.

Beam

A large horizontal structural member of wood or steel.

Bearing wall

A wall which supports the load of the structure above it.

Bevel

Any angle not at 90°. Also, a tool for marking such an angle.

Bird's-mouth

The notch in a rafter that rests on the top plate of a wall.

Box nail

Nail similar to a common nail, but having a smaller diameter shank.

Bridging

Bracing installed in an X-shape between floor joists to stiffen floor and distribute live loads. Also called *cross-bridging*.

Building line

The bottom measurement of a rafter's run, the top being the ridge line; the plumb cut of the bird's-mouth.

Camber

A slight crown or arch in a horizontal structural member.

Cantilever

Any part of a structure that projects beyond its main support and is balanced on it.

Cant strip

A length of lumber with a triangular cross-section used around edges of roofs or decks to help waterproof.

Casing

A piece of wood or metal trim that finishes off the frame of a door or window.

Casing nail

A large finish nail with a cone-shaped head.

Chalk line

A string covered with chalk used for marking straight lines.

Check

A lengthwise crack across the grain in a piece of lumber.

Chisel

A wedge-like, sharp-edged tool used for cutting or shaping wood.

Chord

Any principal member of a truss. In a roof truss the top chord replaces a rafter, and the bottom chord replaces a ceiling joist.

Collar beam

A horizontal board that connects pairs of rafters on opposite roof slopes.

Column

A vertical structural member.

Common nail

Nail used in framing and rough carpentry having a flat head about twice the diameter of its shank.

Corner

Two studs nailed together in an L-shape, used to attach two walls and provide drywall backing.

Cornice

The horizontal projection of a roof overhang at the eaves, consisting of lookout, soffit, and fascia.

Crawl space

The area bounded by foundation walls, first-floor joists, and the ground in a basementless house.

Cricket

A small, sloping structure built on a roof to divert water, usually away from a chimney. Also called a saddle.

Cripple

A short stud installed above or below a horizontal member in a wall opening.

Cripple jack rafter

A rafter which runs between a hip rafter and a valley rafter.

Crowbar

A steel bar usually slightly bent at one or both ends, used as a lever.

Crown

The high point of a piece of lumber with a curve in it.

Cup

Warp across the grain.

d

Abbreviation for penny. The abbreviation comes from the Roman word *denarius,* meaning coin, which the English adapted to penny. It originally referred to the cost of a specific nail per 100. Today it refers only to nail size.

Dead load

The weight of all structures in place.

Dormer

A structure with its own roof projecting from a sloping roof.

Double cheek cut

A two-sided cut that forms a V at the end of some rafters, especially in hip and gambrel roofs.

Eave

The part of a roof that projects beyond its supporting walls.

Face nailing

Nailing at right angles to the surface.

Fascia

A vertical board nailed to the lower ends of rafters that form part of a cornice.

Fire block

A short piece of framing lumber nailed horizontally between joists or studs to partially block the flow of air and, thus, to slow the spread of fire.

Footings

The base, usually poured concrete, on which the foundation wall is built. The footing and foundation wall are often formed and poured as a single unit.

Form

A mold of metal or wood used to shape concrete until it has set.

Foundation

The building's structural support below the first-floor construction. It rests on the footing, and transfers the weight of the building to the soil.

Frame

The wood skeleton of a building. Also called *framing*.

Framer

A person who does rough carpentry.

Framing anchor

A metal device for connecting wood framing members that meet at right angles.

Furring

Strips of wood fastened across studs or joists to a level or plumb nailing surface for finish wall or ceiling material, usually sheetrock. Also called *strapping*.

Gable

The triangular part of an end wall between the eaves and ridge of a house with a peaked roof.

Gable roof

A roof shape characterized by two sections of roof of constant slope that meet at a ridge; peaked roof.

Gambrel roof

A roof shape similar to a gable roof, but with two sections of roof on each side of the ridge, the lower section being steeper than the upper.

Girder

A main horizontal beam of steel or wood.

Grade

1) A designation of quality, especially of lumber and plywood.

2) Ground level. Also the slope of the ground on a building site.

Grain

The direction of fibers in wood.

Gusset

A flat piece of plywood or metal attached to each side of two framing members to tie them together, or strengthen a joint.

Hammer

A tool consisting of a metal head set perpendicular on a handle, used for driving nails.

Header

Any structural wood member used across the ends of an opening to support the cut ends of shortened framing members in a floor, wall, or roof.

Hip

The outside angle where two adjacent sections of roof meet at a diagonal. The opposite of a valley.

Hip rafter

The diagonal rafter which forms a hip.

Hip roof

A roof shape characterized by four or more sections of constant slope, all of which run from a uniform eave height to the ridge.

Jack rafter

A short rafter, usually running between a top plate and a hip rafter or between a ridge and a valley rafter.

Jack stud

A shortened stud supporting the header above a door or window. Also called a trimmer or jamb stud.

Jamb

The side of a window or door opening.

Joint

The line along which two pieces of material meet.

Joist

One of a parallel series of structural members used for supporting a floor or ceiling. Joists are supported by walls, beams, or girders.

Joist hanger

A metal framing anchor for holding joists in position against a rim joist, header or beam.

Kerf

The cut made by a saw blade.

Kneewall

A short wall under a slope, usually in attic space.

Lead framer

Foreman or leader of a crew.

Ledger

A strip of lumber attached to the side of a girder near its bottom edge to support joists. Also, any similar supporting strip.

Level

Perfectly horizontal.

Lightweight plate

A plate that goes under the bottom plate to raise walls for lightweight concrete or gypcrete.

Live load

The total variable weight on a structure. It includes the weights of people, furnishings, snow, and wind.

Lookout

A horizontal framing member between a stud wall and the lower end of a rafter to which the soffit is attached.

Lumber
Wood cut at a sawmill into usable form.

Makeup
Parts of a wall, such as backers, corners, headers, and stud trimmers, which are cut before the wall is spread.

Mansard roof
A type of roof with two slopes on each of four sides, the lower slope much steeper than the upper and ending at a constant eave height.

Mortise
A recess cut into wood.

Mudsill
The lowest plate in a frame wall. It rests on the foundation or slab.

Nail gun
A hand-operated tool powered by compressed air which drives nails.

Nominal size
The rounded-off, simplified dimensional name given to lumber; e.g., a piece of lumber whose actual size is 1½" × 3½" is given the more convenient, nominal designation of 2" × 4".

Nonbearing
A dividing wall that supports none of the structure above it.

Nosing
The rounded front edge of a stair tread that extends over the riser.

On center (O.C.)
Layout spacing designation which refers to distance from the center of one framing member to another.

Overhang
The part of a roof that extends beyond supporting walls.

Parallel
Extending in the same direction equidistant at all points.

Parapet
A low wall or rail at the edge of a balcony or roof.

Partition
An interior wall that divides a building into rooms or areas.

Party wall
A wall between two adjoining living quarters in a multi-family dwelling.

Penny
Word applied to nails to indicate size; abbreviated as "d".

Perpendicular
At right angles to a plane, or flat surface.

Pitch
The slope of a roof.

Plate
A horizontal framing member laid flat.

> **Bottom plate**
> The lowest plate in a wall in the platform framing system, resting on the

subfloor, to which the lower ends of studs are nailed.

Double plate
The uppermost plate in a frame wall that has two plates at the top. Also called a cap or rafter plate.

Sill plate
The structural member, attached to the top of the foundation, that supports the floor structure. Also called a sill or mudsill.

Top plate
The framing member nailed across the upper ends of studs and beneath the double plate.

Platform framing
A method of construction in which wall framing is built on and attached to a finished box sill. Joists and studs are not fastened together as in balloon and braced framing.

Plumb
Straight up and down, perfectly vertical.

Plumb and line
The process of straightening all the walls so they are vertical and straight from end to end.

Plumb cut
Any cut in a piece of lumber, such as at the upper end of a common rafter, that will be plumb when the piece is in its final position.

Purlin
The horizontal framing members in a gambrel roof between upper and lower rafters.

Rabbet
A groove cut in or near the edge of a piece of lumber to receive the edge of another piece.

Rafter
One of a series of main structural members which form a roof.

Rake
The finish wood member running parallel to the roof slope at the gable end.

Reveal
The surface left exposed when one board is fastened over another; the edge of the upper set slightly back from the edge of the lower.

Ridge
The horizontal board to which the top ends of rafters are attached.

Rim joist
Joist which forms the perimeter of a floor framing system.

Rise
1) In a roof, the vertical distance between the top of the double plate and the point where a line, drawn through the edge of the double plate and parallel to the roof's slope, intersects the center line of the ridgeboard.
2) In a stairway, the vertical height of the entire stairway measured from floor to floor.

Riser

The vertical board between two stair treads.

Roof sheathing

Material, usually plywood, laid flat on roof trusses or rafters to form the roof.

Rough opening (R.O.)

Any opening formed by the framing members to accommodate doors or windows.

Rout

To cut out by gouging.

Run

1) In a roof with a ridge, the horizontal distance between the edge of the rafter plate (building line) and the center line of the ridgeboard.
2) In a stairway, the horizontal distance between the top and bottom risers plus the width of one tread.

Scaffold

Any temporary working platform and the structure to support it.

Scribe

To mark for an irregular cut.

Seat cut

The horizontal cut in a bird's-mouth that rests on the double plate.

Shed roof

A roof that slopes in only one direction.

Shim

A thin piece of material, often tapered (such as a wood shingle) inserted between building materials for the purpose of straightening or making their surfaces flush at a joint.

Sill

1) A sill plate.
2) The structural member forming the bottom of a rough opening for a door or window. Also, the bottom member of a door or window frame.

Single cheek cut

A bevel cut at the end of a rafter, especially in hip and gambrel roofs.

Sleeper

Lumber laid on a concrete floor as a nailing base for wood flooring.

Slope

The pitch of a roof, expressed as inches of rise per 12" of run.

Soffit

The underside of a projection, such as a cornice.

Solid bridging

Blocking between joists cut from the same lumber as the joists themselves and used to stiffen the floor.

Spacer

Any piece of material used to maintain a permanent space between two members.

Span

The distance between structural supports, measured horizontally.

Speed square

A triangle-shaped tool used for marking perpendicular and angled lines.

Square

1) At 90° or a right angle.
2) The process of marking and cutting at a right angle.
3) Any of several tools for marking at right angles and for laying out structural members for cutting or positioning.
4) A measure of roofing and some siding materials equal to 100 square feet of coverage.

Stair

A single step.

Stair nuts

Two screw clamps that are attached to a framing square for marking stair stringers.

Stairway

A flight of stairs, made up of stringers, risers, and treads.

Stairwell

The opening in a floor for a stairway.

Stickers

Strips of scrap wood used to create an air space between layers of lumber.

Stop

In general, any device or member that prevents movement.

Story pole

A length of wood marked off and used for repetitive layout or to accurately transfer measurements.

Stringer

In stairway construction, the diagonal member that supports treads and to which risers are attached.

Structural

Adjective generally synonymous with "framing."

Stud

The main vertical framing member in a wall to which finish material or other covering is attached.

Subfloor sheathing

The rough floor, usually plywood, laid across floor joists and under finish flooring.

Tail

The part of a rafter which extends beyond the double plate.

Tail joist

A shortened joist that butts against a header.

Tape

A measure of coiled flexible steel.

Template
A full-sized pattern.

Threshold
The member at the bottom of a door between the jambs.

Toenailing
To drive a nail at an angle to join two pieces of wood.

Tongue
The shorter and narrower of the two legs of a framing square.

Tool pouch
Pouch worn around the waist for holding tools and nails.

Tread
The horizontal platform of a stair.

Trimmer
The structural member on the side of a framed rough opening to narrow or stiffen the opening. Also the shortened stud (jack stud) which supports a header in a door or window opening.

Truss
An assembly for bridging a broad span, most commonly used in roof construction.

Utility knife
A hand-held knife with a razor-like blade, commonly used to cut drywall, sharpen pencils, etc.

Valley
The inside angle where two adjacent sections of a roof meet at a diagonal. The opposite of a hip.

Valley rafter
A diagonal rafter which forms a valley.

Wall puller
A tool used for aligning walls.

Wall sheathing
Material, usually plywood, attached to studs to form the outside wall and provide structural strength.

Wane
A defect in lumber caused at the mill by sawing too close to the outside edge of a log and leaving an edge either incomplete or covered with bark.

Warp
Any variation from straight in a piece of lumber; bow, cup, crook, twist.

Western framing
Platform framing.

Worm-drive saw
A circular power saw turned by a worm-gear drive. It is somewhat heavier and produces more torque on the blade than a standard circular saw.

For Reading and Reference

APA. *GluLam in Residential Construction*. APA, 1997.

Badzinski, Stanley, Jr. *Roof Framing*. Englewood Cliffs, NJ: Prentice Hall, Inc., 1976.

Baily, Robert F. *Pocket Size Carpenter's Helper*. Rs. Wood and Co., 1986.

Ball, John E. *Audel's Carpenters and Builders Library* (Four volumes). Indianapolis, IN: Audel/Sams, 1977.

Blackburn, Graham. *Illustrated Basic Carpentry*. Boston: Little, Brown, 1977.

Burbank, Nelson L. "House Carpentry Simplified." *The Journal of Light Construction*, 1992.

Canadian Home Builder's Association (CHBA). *Builder's Manual*. CHBA, 1989.

Cascol, Inc. *Unequal Pitch Rafter Length & Guide*. Cascol, Inc., 1993.

Chadwich, Charley, G., et al. *Wall Framing*. American Association for Vocational Instructional Materials, 1989.

Currie, Mark. *Rough Framing Carpentry*. Carlsbad, CA: Craftsman Book Company, 1993

Earthquake Engineering Research Institute (EERI) and the International Conference of Building Officials (ICBO). *Resisting the Forces of Earthquakes,* (video). EERI & ICBO, 2000.

Ehrlich, Jeffrey and Mannheimer, March. *The Carpenter's Manifesto*. Henry Holt and Company, Inc., 1990.

Feirer, John and Gilbert Hutchings. *Carpentry and Building Construction*. Peoria, IL: Chas. A. Bennett Co., Inc., 1981.

Fine Homebuilding Builder's Library. *Frame Carpentry*. Newton, CT: Taunton Publications, 1988.

Gross, Marshall. *Roof Framing*. Carlsbad, CA: Craftsman Book Company, 1989.

Hageman, Jack M. *Contractor's Guide to the Building Code*. Carlsbad, CA: Craftsman Book Company, 1983.

Huth, Harry C. *Practical Problems in Mathematics for Carpenters*. Delmar Publishers, Inc., 1985.

Journal of Light Construction. SF499 Residential Structure Framing. *The Journal of Light Construction.*

Journal of Light Construction. "Advanced Framing." *The Journal of Light Construction*, 1992.

Koel, Leonard. *Carpentry*. Homewood, IL: American Technical Publishers, Inc., 1985.

Locke, Jim. *The Apple Corps Guide to the Well-Built House*. Boston: Houghton Mifflin, 1988.

Maguire, Byron W. *Carpentry in Commercial Construction*. Carlsbad, CA: Craftsman Book Company, 1988.

Maguire, Byron W. *Carpentry for Residential Construction*. Carlsbad, CA: Craftsman Book Company, 1987.

Maguire, Byron W. *Carpentry Framing and Finishing* (second edition). Englewood Cliffs, NJ: Prentice Hall, 1989.

Mussell, Barry D. *Roof Framer's Bible: The Complete Pocket Reference to Roof Framing*. Carlsbad, CA: Craftsman Book Company, 1996.

National Lumber Manufacturers Association. *Manual for House Framing*. Washington, D.C.: National Forest Products Association, 1961.

R.S. Means. *Residential & Light Commercial Construction Standards*. Kingston, MA: R.S. Means Company, Inc., 1998.

Reed, Mortimer. *Residential Carpentry*. New York: John Wiley and Sons, Inc., 1980.

Riechers, A.F.J. *Full Length of Roof Framer*. Buccaneer Books, 1995.

Sherwood, Gerald E., and Robert C. Stroh, *Wood-Frame House Construction*. Carlsbad, CA: Craftsman Book Company, 1993.

Spence, William Perkins. *Residential Framing: A Homebuilder's Construction Guide*. Sterling Publications, 1993.

Sunset Books. *Basic Carpentry Illustrated*. Menlo Park, CA: Lane Publishing Co., 1995.

Syvanen, Bob. *Carpentry: Some Tricks of the Trade from an Old-Style Carpenter*. Charlotte, NC: East Woods/Fast and McMillan, 1982.

Taunton Press. *Frame Carpentry*. Newton, CT: Taunton Press, 1988.

Taunton Press. *More Frame Carpentry*. Newton, CT: Taunton Press, 1993.

Tetrault, Jeanne. *The Women's Carpentry Book*. New York: Anchor/Doubleday, 1980.

Thallon, Rob. *Graphic Guide to Frame Construction: Details for Builders and Designers*. Newton, CT: Taunton Press, 2000.

Tood, Ken. *Carpentry Layout*. Carlsbad, CA: Craftsman Book Company, 1988.

Truss Plate Institute (TPI). *Commentary and Recommendations for Handling, Installing & Bracing Metal Plate Connected Wood Trusses* (HIB-91). TPI, 1991.

Wagner, John D. *House Framing*. Upper Saddle River, NJ: Creative Homeowner Press, 1998.

Wagner, Willis. *Modern Carpentry*. S. Holland, IL: Goodheart-Willcox, 1976.

Wahlfeldt, Bette. *Woodframe House Building: An Illustrated Guide*. Blue Ridge Summit, PA: Tab, 1988.

Wilson, J. Douglas. *Practical House Carpentry*. New York: McGraw-Hill, 1973.

Index

W